The Complete Wedding Book

The Complete Wedding Book

JILL THOMAS

World's Work Ltd.

Text copyright © 1983 Jill Thomas

Published by World's Work Ltd,
The Windmill Press,
Kingswood, Tadworth, Surrey

ISBN 0 437 17405 0 World's Work

Filmset by Northumberland Press Ltd, Gateshead
Printed in England by
Richard Clay (The Chaucer Press) Ltd,
Bungay, Suffolk

Contents

Planning

It cannot be stressed too much how important it is to plan a wedding carefully and to think every aspect through thoroughly. Good planning and organisation not only saves money, but time as well.

COUNTING THE COST

Before booking a wedding it is important to think about the end, when you actually get to the wedding day and everything has to be paid for. This is the time to 'cut your coat according to your cloth'. In order to assist you with this, each section of the book will give you a costing chart so that you can work out how much each part of your wedding is going to cost. On page 43 you will find an overall costing chart. You will note that at the end of this chart there is an additional 20% contingency fund added. It is important that you include this to cover any extras you may not have thought of and to allow for rising prices.

7

APPROACHING PARENTS FOR FINANCIAL ASSISTANCE

At one time it was always the custom for the Bride's parents to pay the lion's share of the expenses. Today, however, with more young people living independently away from home, and especially in the case of second weddings, the Bride and Groom often feel that they must pay for their own wedding. With most weddings, whether first or second, or even subsequent, both sets of parents usually expect to invite their relatives and some of their long standing friends, and they therefore realise that they should, at least, make a contribution to the cost of the food and drink at the reception. When young couples try to arrange and pay for everything themselves, parents often feel hurt and left out, so it is a good idea to approach them to find out how many guests each set of parents would like to invite and, having established that figure, how much of a contribution they are prepared to make.

FOLLOWING TRADITIONS

Traditionally the Bride's family pays for everything, except the bouquets for the Bride and Bridesmaids and fees and expenses at the church which are usually paid for by the Groom. Where this is the case, the Groom's family may feel that they have to restrict the number of people they invite. One way to prevent this situation arising is for the Bride's mother and Groom's mother to arrange a coffee party where they can discuss with the Bride how many guests it would be reasonable for the Groom's family to invite. If the Groom's family is really huge and the Groom's parents feel that everyone should be invited, then it is at this stage that they should offer to pay a proportion of the expenses.

SAVING

Building Societies

A building society is a good place for an engaged couple to entrust their savings, especially if they are also proposing to save the deposit for a home of their own. It is advisable to shop around and find out who is offering the best deal. Do not assume that one society is as good as another. Usually building societies offer better interest rates if you save a set amount per month with restricted drawing periods.

If you decide to tie your money up in order to gain a higher interest rate, remember you must have a 'Contingency Fund'. A good idea is to work out the maximum figure you can save each month and have two-thirds of that figure put into a "High Interest Account" and the other third put into a normal share account.

Building societies like regular savers, even if you do propose eventually to withdraw your complete savings in a lump sum. It can be that when you want your mortgage the building society has run low on the fund it uses for this purpose, but a regular saving record definitely will help when applying for a mortgage to another building society. When it comes to arranging a mortgage, if the building society you have been saving with cannot help you, then let your estate agent or solicitor find you a building society which can.

Banks

Banks are very good because they usually allow fairly easy access to your savings.

Do compare their interest rates with building societies carefully. There are times when banks offer better interest rates. Banks do allow mortgages too and if you have a healthy deposit account with them, then, again, they are obviously more enthusiastic about granting a mortgage. Do be careful about a mortgage with a bank, though, because it can be that if at a later date you approach the bank for a car loan, or something else, you will have used up your borrowing facilities with them.

A combination of building society and bank saving would appear to be the best solution, in order to keep your options open. A 'High Interest Account' with the building society and deposit account with a bank together with a current account, so that you have a cheque book with which to pay your bills when you come to your wedding day would seem to be the ideal arrangement.

Credit

Generally speaking most wedding suppliers do not allow credit, although some will allow you to pay weekly, before the wedding, so that everything is paid for by the time you collect it. But, remember, if you are paying weekly, you could just as easily be paying this amount into one of your deposit accounts enabling you to pay your supplier at the end the same amount, whilst gaining interest on your account.

CREDIT CARDS

Some wedding dress suppliers, caterers, especially restaurants, photographers and florists take credit cards. If you are a credit card holder, or can apply for a credit card and you feel that it is a good idea to use credit in this instance then it is worth shopping round to find out who accepts credit cards. However, do watch out for interest rates – they can work out to be very expensive.

PERSONAL LOANS AND OVERDRAFTS

Some banks, especially if you are a long standing customer, may allow you a bank loan to help with wedding or honeymoon expenses and generally speaking it is cheaper to obtain a small loan from the bank than to use credit cards as the interest rates are lower.

WHEN TO BOOK

Church	Immediately you are engaged, or have made the decision to get married, providing you do not intend to have a long engagement.

Registry Office	Registry Offices do not take bookings longer than three months in advance.
Reception Hall /Hotel /Restaurant	Immediately you have booked the church or registry office. When you are getting married in a registry office and you want your reception in a place which you know gets booked up early, especially if you are getting married in the summer, then it is a good idea to book your reception tentatively. Registry office weddings usually take place during the week, but if you are arranging a church blessing to follow, then make sure the proprietors of the company handling your wedding reception understand that you cannot confirm the date and time until three months before the wedding and that any deposits paid would be transferable to another date, if necessary.
Caterer	Immediately you have booked your reception hall.
Photographer	Give him as much notice as possible. Some sources say three months in advance, but if you want a specific photographer, who is renowned for the quality of his work then as soon as you know your date and time you should book (see photography).
Cars	Book as early as possible, especially if you want a Rolls Royce or carriage and pair. Remember the lower priced estimates tend to get accepted first, so you may end up paying more for the same service by booking late.

Cake	Ideally a cake should stand for six to nine months before it is iced, but at least a month's notice should be given. This is not to say that some confectioners will not take shorter notice.
Flowers	As soon as the Bridesmaid's and Bride's outfits are chosen, although it is a good idea to have a word with a florist beforehand, to get an idea of what information she may require and how much it is going to cost.

WHEN YOU PAY

With nearly everything you will find it necessary to pay a deposit when you book. The balance is expected either about a fortnight before the wedding or on the actual wedding day. Generally speaking deposits are not refundable if you cancel, although if the date is changed for some reason, most suppliers will transfer the deposit.

GETTING PEOPLE THERE

It is not the Bride or Groom's responsibility to get people to their wedding. Remember it is your day and if you are having to rush around after other people you will be too tired to enjoy it. By all means arrange for friends to collect elderly relatives from the station, but if they cannot do so, make arrangements for taxis, etc. to collect guests who cannot drive to the church. Whatever you do encourage guests to go straight to the church, *not* to the Bride's house. Most likely the photographer will be coming to the Bride's house to take photographs and Bridesmaids will be there and if there are young Bridesmaids, then probably their parents as well. Bridesmaids who have to travel a very long way may have to change at the Bride's house, or may even have stayed overnight, involving the possible use of camp beds, etc. You need to have a very large house with a great number of bedrooms to enable the Bride to change and get ready in a calm atmosphere, let alone with long forgotten relatives turning up, wanting to see the Bride and go into long dissertations over how they remember her as a child, so do tactfully impress on guests that you will look forward to seeing them at the church and not at your house.

OVERNIGHT GUESTS

It is vital to make sure that the Bride and Groom are staying in the vicinity of the church on the night before the wedding. This may seem obvious, but all too many people try to travel too far to get to the church on the day of the wedding and suffer as a result of this.

Recently we were photographing a three o'clock wedding and we arrived at the Bride's house at two o'clock to take photographs of the Bride, her Bridesmaids and her mother and father. We photographed the bride leaving the house and then proceeded to the church to await the arrival of the Groom. At ten to three the Bridesmaids arrived, at three o'clock the Bride arrived, but there was no sign of the Groom or Best Man, so the Bride went for a little drive. At 3.05 there was still no Groom. The Bride started to fret. At 3.10 there was still no Groom and no Vicar. The Bridesmaids were getting fidgety and the Bride started to cry. The Best Man hadn't arrived yet either. At 3.20 a taxi drew up and out jumped the Groom wearing jeans and a tee shirt covered in grease, accompanied by the Vicar, from some fifty miles away. His car had broken down. He rushed off to change, by which time the Best Man had arrived. They eventually went into church at 3.50.

This was not a total disaster as there were no other weddings at that church that day, but some churches conduct one wedding ceremony every hour and I dread to think what would have happened if there had been a four o'clock and a five o'clock wedding that day, as legally you must be married before six o'clock. The point of this story is that as long as you have a Bride and Groom and Vicar and preferably the Best Man, then the wedding can go ahead without anyone else being present.

It is imperative that both the Bride and Groom get a good night's sleep and everyone else's comfort should be sacrificed to that end. Next in line of importance are the two sets of parents, particularly if they are arranging the catering as they will have an inordinate amount of work to do the next day, which will fall flat if they are tired out through, say, sleeping on the floor in order to let great aunt Ethel sleep in their bed because of her arthritis.

If either the Bride or the Groom and their family have a long way to travel and they have no relatives living reasonably close to the Church with whom they might stay, and there are no friends who can put them up, then it might be a good idea to economise elsewhere and allow expenses for an hotel or boarding house for the Groom, Best Man and the Groom's parents.

Guests staying with the Bride's Parents

As stated above, we generally feel that this is not a good idea. Guests arriving the day before the wedding expect to be entertained as well as put up for the night and all this involves a great deal of work and expense.

Guests staying with friends of the Bride and Groom

When asked, friends and relatives are often quite happy to accommodate other friends or relatives coming to a wedding on the night before the wedding and are usually delighted to be asked. When the Bride and Groom have left for their honeymoon, then it is usually possible for such guests to move in with the Bride's parents for the night of the wedding and a few days after if this is considered desirable. If you do have to arrange accommodation do try to match the various age groups. Great aunt Ethel would be much happier staying with mum's friend in her sixties, than the Bride's best friend of some nineteen years, who herself has only recently married. The Groom's friend of some twenty-one years will be only too delighted to stay with the Bride's friend! If great aunt Ethel lives close to hand, then perhaps the Groom's parents can stay with her (giving her something to do and keeping her out of everyone's hair) and the Groom and Best Man can perhaps stay with the Bride's married friend. It is not considered appropriate for single men to stay with single women (unless a sister) on the night before their wedding.

Hotels

Hotels frequently do a special 'Wedding Offer', especially if the wedding reception is being held there, with large discounts for guests staying the night before and the night after the wedding, and most hotels do a special wedding night offer for the Bride and Groom whether or not the reception is being held there and it is worth finding out if hotels give a quantity discount for a large number of guests staying there as a block booking. It is a good idea to telephone several hotels for their terms.

GUESTS ARRIVING ON THE DAY

At the Bride's House

As previously mentioned this should be discouraged at all costs.

At the Church

At most weddings there are people travelling long distances to areas with which they are unfamiliar. If this is so, please ensure that they are given instructions how to get there: a photostated map with arrows and estimated times, etc. for drivers and train and bus schedules with taxi rank numbers for guests coming 'on foot'.

Please ensure that guests are aware of any local peculiarities. Once the Groom's parents missed nearly all the ceremony because the church was at the end of a high street, which was congested with traffic on a Saturday. A fact of which they were totally unaware because on the previous evening they had driven from their hotel to see the Bride's family, passing the church on their way. It had only taken them ten minutes then, but on the Saturday when the road was congested, it took over half an hour. Also as most churches are in the centre of the town or are only approached through the centre of the town, do check with the police, well in advance of your wedding, for local activities such as carnivals, parades, demonstrations which might cause delays and then check again a week before.

DUTIES OF IMPORTANT PEOPLE

Although the progress of the ceremony is covered under the section 'Ceremony' on page 217, the respective duties of various important persons involved in a wedding all need to be highly organised, and we therefore feel that certain aspects of their duties need covering in the 'Planning' stage.

Best Man
The Best Man's duty is to ensure that the Groom gets to the church on time (half an hour to twenty minutes before the Ceremony). He looks after the requirements of the Groom and perhaps even more important keeps the ring in his pocket to produce at the right moment in the service. The Best Man also has to make a speech. Bearing this in mind it is better to choose someone who can take the responsibility and is not too shy to make a speech. Anyone who says they could not possibly make a speech, but would be delighted to accept the job on the understanding that they will not have to make a speech, is saying that they will accept the easy part, but not the difficult, which means that they are not a suitable choice for the job. It could be better to ask a young Uncle with a sense of responsibility (the Best Man also usually carries the cash to pay for anything which has to be paid on the day and ensures that everyone is paid) than a friend or brother who might panic on the day. Also someone with a good sense of humour, who can give light touches to his speech is a good idea. Speeches will be covered in a later section. The Best Man's

speech is always looked forward to by the Bride and Groom and all the guests, so it is important that the Best Man feels capable of putting it over. The Best Man is also in charge of the Ushers who hand out service sheets and show the guests to their seats at the Church and at the Reception. If there is a toast-master the Best Man liaises with him, if not then it is up to the Best Man to make any announcements regarding the speeches and cutting of the cake. It is up to the Best Man to look after the Groom's clothes for his wedding day, and any transport arrangements. He drives the Groom to the church. He ensures that the Bride and Groom leave for their honeymoon on time and that their car (their own or a taxi) is available when they are ready to leave. He also makes sure that all the documentation necessary for the honeymoon is on the Groom when he leaves, i.e. tickets, passports, etc. After the Bride and Groom have left, he takes charge of the Bridegroom's clothes and the transportation of the wedding presents.

Bridesmaids

Many Brides these days choose to have just a couple of small children for Bridesmaids but we feel that this is not a good idea. Also it should be borne in mind that very small children are just not happy standing still for half an hour during the ceremony and may fret immediately their mother leaves for the church without them. Very small children can also get tearful about having their photographs taken and when you think that you could well have spent upwards of thirty to forty pounds on out-fitting them, then not to be able to have a photograph of them does make it seem like a terrible waste. Remember the photo-grapher does not have an unlimited amount of time to wait for a small Bridesmaid to stop fretting and crying. If you do have a Bridesmaid who starts to cry, then do not worry if she isn't included in the photography session, just ask her mother to take her away and comfort her.

Generally speaking, children under the age of five are too young to be Bridesmaids or Pageboys, although we have known of children much younger who have behaved impeccably. However, it is not until they reach the age of about eight that they can be relied upon.

The Chief Bridesmaid should be an adult and her duties to the Bride are similar to those of the Best Man to the Groom. She helps the Bride to dress (and not the reverse as is frequently the case). She holds the Bride's flowers in church. She meets the Bride from the car and carries her train and veil out and arranges them to perfection. At the reception she fetches and carries any needs of the Bride and, if necessary, helps her out of her wedding dress and into her 'going away' outfit. Although it frequently happens, it is wrong for the Bridesmaids to change out of their dresses into their own clothes for the evening reception. They should wear their dresses and headdresses all day and evening.

Basically, the same rule follows as for the Best Man that it is better to have someone who is aware of the honour of being a Bridesmaid and is prepared to carry out all the functions required, rather than someone who is reluctant or nervous about the responsibility.

Ushers

Ushers are an excellent idea. For one thing they do not cost any extra (all they have to define them is a single red carnation instead of a single white one) and at least one Usher from each side is required and should be family. They hand out hymn books, prayer books, or orders of service, buttonholes, show guests to their seats at the church and at the reception and can add a great deal of organisation to the whole proceedings. It is also the duty of one of the Ushers to accompany the Bride's mother to her seat, as she is unescorted. One of the Ushers should also escort any other unescorted lady to her seat.

Bride's Parents

The Bride's mother helps her daughter to dress and most mothers like to fix their daughter's headdress and pull the veil over before leaving with the Bridesmaids, thus leaving the Bride alone with her father (normally a very emotional moment for everyone) and the Bridesmaids should get into the car leaving the Bride's mother alone with her husband and daughter for just a quick goodbye, as the next time she speaks to her, her daughter will be a married woman. The Bride's father accompanies his daughter to the church and takes her on his arm down the aisle where he 'gives her away'. He makes a speech at the reception and this should not be avoided. The Bride's father's speech is something she will remember for the rest of her life.

Where there is no Bride's father, then the next closest male relative is usually chosen. A brother is not usually a good idea; he would probably serve better as an Usher, as he has not necessarily known the Bride all her life. A close Uncle will do. Sometimes, if the Bride's mother has remarried or if she has a close friend then he can be chosen to take the place of the Bride's father. However, there is absolutely no need of this unless the Bride is parentless. It is quite acceptable for the Bride's *mother* to give her away and, especially if the Bride's father has died, we feel, is probably more appropriate and will avoid giving offence to the father's relatives, when selecting an Uncle or where there is a second husband. Alternatively, it is not necessary to have the 'giving away' ceremony in the service at all.

Groom's Parents

The Groom's Parents do not have to do very much. Obviously if they are making a financial contribution, then it is a nice gesture to involve them in arrangements like the seating plan. However, apart from going into the vestry for the signing of the register and sitting on the top table, there is no traditional position for them. They should arrive at the church shortly before their son and his Best Man. However, having said this, we feel a lot of trouble can be avoided by asking the Groom's mother her opinion on certain issues and perhaps taking her with you on some of the shopping trips for wedding attire. Even if she does not accept the invitation, she may secretly feel a whole lot better about the situation if she is asked.

If the Groom's father is a public speaker or likes making speeches, then it is quite acceptable for him to make a speech at the reception too. It is better to let him speak rather than have him feeling left out as well.

If there is no Groom's father, then one of the Ushers accompanies the Groom's mother to the church and escorts her to her seat, before assuming his position outside the church and carrying on with his other duties.

Divorced Parents

The fact is that they simply bury the hatchet for the sake of their son or daughter, no matter how acrimonious relationships may be between them. If it is the Bride's parents who are divorced, then the Bride's mother just accepts her father at her house and leaves as soon as possible and the Bride's father takes it upon himself to behave impeccably, arriving as late as possible, trying to time his arrival at the Bride's mother's house with her departure with the Bridesmaids, thus avoiding prolonged contact if they find it hard to be nice to one another. He accompanies his ex-wife to the vestry and when the company 'recess', then he takes the Groom's mother's arm and Bride's mother accompanies the Groom's father and it is, perhaps, better if they sit this way at the reception.

If it is the Groom's parents who are divorced, then they may arrive at the church separately; the Usher accompanies the Groom's mother to her seat, but they sit together in church.

New partners sit at the back of the church with 'friends'. Remember the Prince and Princess of Wales' wedding! New partners are seated at the Reception away from the top table but together with some relatives they know.

USE OF A DIARY AND SCHEDULES

Immediately you decide to get married BUY A DIARY, not a handbag size one, but a large desk diary. Enter everything into the diary immediately you start to make arrangements, even if it is months in advance. If the caterer says he will ring you a month before the wedding, make a note in your diary a month before the wedding that he should speak to you by then.

If someone promises to deliver something on Friday, make a note on that day. When you make appointments to see people, make a note in the diary. When you book the hairdressers, make a note in the diary two months before the date of the wedding to start seeing a hairdresser (see 'Appearance') and when you see him, make the rest of your appointments, including your wedding day one and put the times in your diary.

Remember when you book caterers, photographers, etc. they will tell you a date by which they expect you to provide information about numbers, etc. and when they will invoice you. These preliminary discussions can take place months before your wedding day and you will forget what they say if you do not make notes.

Make a special schedule of the four weeks before the wedding and write daily instructions of things to do. On each Sunday make a separate schedule for the whole week, drawing on your diary and monthly schedules. On the Sunday of the week before the wedding, make a schedule of the week, carefully checking times of appointments and remember if you do not achieve what you want to on one day, to carry it forward to the next day. It is, therefore, best to try and achieve as much as possible early in each week, possibly on Monday, so that if you hit problems you have time to sort them out without having to carry work over into the next week. If chores start mounting up you will find yourself rushing around on the day of the wedding.

Communication is one of the most important parts of life and good communication not only improves relationships in arranging a wedding, but once mastered will enable you to cope with any situation which may occur throughout your married life.

When a decision is made on any issue, make sure everyone knows about it. It is a good idea to keep a note-pad in your pocket or handbag and if when chatting with your mother over coffee you decide that it would be lovely to have the Bridesmaids in

pink and lilac, write it down. The next day, contact the Bridesmaids and get their views. Write down any questions that your
mother asks you to ask the Groom's mother about the needs of
elderly or handicapped relatives who might be coming to the
wedding, for example. If you do not write things down you will
forget them as you have so much to think about. If it is something
you promise to do at the weekend or the next day, then put it
in the diary and check the diary every day. If the Bride and her
mother are handling things between them then divide the page
of the diary into two and make separate entries. Using this system
each has her own individual duties, but both can keep an eye
on all the arrangements.

WEDDING PRESENT LIST

Please *do* make a wedding gift list. These days people expect it.
Think it out clearly and make sure that no misinterpretation can
be put on what you request. A lot of the large stores offer Wedding
List facilities, where your guests can go into the local branch and
be informed of what you have requested and purchase all of an
item, or even part, so that maybe two Aunts can get together
and buy you something more expensive that you need and prevent
you from ending up with dozens of glasses and drawers full of
linen. A bit of organisation at this stage can make the whole thing
worth while. Please do not make statements like 'I don't want
presents, I just want people to come and enjoy my wedding'.
Everyone knows and accepts this, but at the same time wishes
to express their delight at your marriage and to give a small item
towards your future home and life, so that when you use it you
will think of them.

If you are given an excess of one particular item it is easier
to exchange it for something different if the presents come from
chain stores like Marks and Spencers; also the gift will not have
to be taken back to the same store from which it was purchased
as most areas have one of their branches.

Accept gifts of money graciously and remember that sometimes elderly people give money because they are unable to have a good scout round the shops and batchelors (especially older ones) find choosing a present difficult, so do make sure you thank them enthusiastically. Try to buy something you know they would like you to have and always tell them what you have bought.

We give an example of a wedding list and the details to put on it, but if your home is already well established you could always ask for gardening tools or plants and shrubs.

Also when making up a wedding list make sure that you think of items for under £2.00 (for children and people who are not coming to your wedding, but would like to give you a small gift), items under £5.00 things under £10.00 and then go up in tens to £50.00 and then the big items – you never know. Sometimes people might not be able to buy you a new washing machine or dish-washer but they might know of a good second-hand one and either buy it for you or let you know of its where-abouts.

If you can, photostat your wedding list, and keep copies by you to refer to when people ask for help.

WEDDING PRESENT LIST

Item	Made By	Model/Design	Colour	Available from	Gift from
Kitchen					
Cooker					
Refrigerator					
Washing machine					
Spin/tumble dryer					
Microwave oven					
Electric mixer					
Liquidiser					
Slow cooker					
Pressure cooker					
Saucepans					
Deep fry					
Frying pan					
Coffee percolator					
Kettle					
Dishwasher					
Knife sharpener					
Electric carving knife					
Mixing bowls					
Casserole set					
Baking tins					
Roasting pans					
Carving set: knives					
dish					
Bread knife					
Toaster					
Tea towels					
Corkscrew					
Infra red grill					
Plate drainer					
Plastic bowl and					
sink accessory set					
Rolling pin					
Grapefruit knife					
Cheese knife & board					

WEDDING PRESENT LIST

Item	Made By	Model/ Design	Colour	Available from	Gift from
Trays					
Vegetable rack					
Kitchen scissors					
Bread bin					
Can opener					
Sieve					
Colander					
Spice rack					
Iron					
Ironing board					
Chopping board					
Set of canisters					
Dining Room					
Hostess trolley					
Dinner service					
Coffee set					
Tea set					
Completer set					
Cutlery set					
Sherry glasses					
Wine glasses					
Champagne glasses					
Brandy glasses					
Liqueur glasses					
Whisky glasses					
Water set					
Beer glasses					
Tablecloth					
Table napkins					
Place mats					
Coasters					
Cruet					
Table and chairs					
Serving spoons					
Salad bowl and servers					

WEDDING PRESENT LIST

Item	Made By	Model Design	Colour	Available from	Gift from
Fruit set					
Mugs					
Egg cups					
Candle holders					
Rose bowl					
Vases					
Bedrooms					
Double bed					
Single bed					
Bedspread					
Continetal quilt					
Quilt cover					
Fitted sheet					
Pillow cases					
Pillows					
Electric blanket					
Bedside lamps					
Teamaker					
Clock/radio					
Sitting room					
Settee					
Chairs					
Coffee table					
Television					
Video cassette recorder					
Carpet					
Scatter rugs					
Cushions					
Stereo					
Radio					
Clock					
Ashtrays					
Occasional tables					
Ornaments					
Drinks cabinet					

WEDDING PRESENT LIST

Item	Made By	Model/ Design	Colour	Available from	Gift from
Wine rack					
Pot plant					
Bathroom					
Bath mat					
Bathroom cabinet					
Mirror					
Bathroom scales					
Bath towels					
Hand towels					
Face flannels					
Linen basket					
Clothes drier					
Clothes horse					
Storage jars					
Electric shower					
Shower curtain					
Garden					
Shed					
Spade					
Fork					
Hoe					
Rake					
Trowel					
Hand fork					
Lawn mower					
Barbecue					
Deck chairs					
Sun loungers					
Table and chairs					
Sun umbrella					
Trees					
Shrubs					
Roses					
Bulbs and corms					

WEDDING PRESENT LIST					
Item	Made By	Model/ Design	Colour	Available from	Gift from
Car					
Car rugs					
Cassette player					
Maps					
Miscellaneous					
Wedding album					
Framed wedding photograph					
Books: Cookery					
Garden					
Home					
Maintenance					
Law					
Health					

Naming the Day

TIME OF THE YEAR

The timing of your wedding is one of the most important things to think about. In England it is legal to get married on any day of the year except Christmas Day. Of course, Registry Offices do not open on Saturday afternoons or Sundays. However, when booking a wedding a few things should be taken into account.

Today many couples marry at a time of the year which is financially convenient to them, either because they are buying a house which will become available at that time, or because they will have saved up enough money to afford the wedding. March and September used to be popular months for weddings as there were tax advantages in getting married in those months, but this no longer applies as legislation has removed these advantages.

Many churches do not permit flowers to decorate the church during Lent (between Shrove Tuesday and Easter) and Advent (about a month before Christmas) nor the use of the bells.

When booking your wedding to fit in with the availability of your new home, it is worth bearing in mind that completion of contracts does not always go according to plan. If buying an established property there will probably be a 'line of exchange' and there can be all sorts of problems further up the line, which delay the completion. If it is a new property, then there can be delays with building work.

Spring and Summer weddings are usually the most popular as there is a greater choice of flowers and there is always the hope of warmer, more reliable weather.

May is considered a bad luck month for a wedding. The old proverb goes 'Marry in May, Rue the day'.

DAY OF THE WEEK

Most weddings take place on a Saturday, although people with businesses to run, frequently prefer a Sunday wedding. This can complicate things for guests who have to travel a long way and have to be at work again the next day, but with longer holidays generally allocated now, many people find it quite easy to take a day off work to attend a family wedding.

Friday weddings are also popular, especially for registry office weddings. As registry offices are not open on Saturday afternoons, it either means having a very early wedding and an afternoon reception, or else having a break between the ceremony and the reception in the evening, leaving the guests to fend for themselves in the meantime, which is not very practical, especially when people have travelled a long way to a wedding. So Friday afternoon becomes an alternative, so that guests only need to take an afternoon off work and the reception can be held directly after the ceremony.

THE TIME OF DAY

Historically, weddings always took place, by law, in the mornings, followed by a wedding breakfast, but during this century the time was extended to 3 p.m. and now you can legally get married on any day between 8 a.m. and 6 p.m. However the most popular time for a wedding is 3 p.m. as this gives time for a wedding breakfast, followed by an evening reception. Some people prefer 5 p.m. and give a buffet meal afterwards, feeling that this economises on the drinks bill. It should be borne in mind that it is usually about one and a half hours after the time of the wedding before you and your guests will be ready to sit down for the breakfast.

However, if you plan to have a winter wedding, remember that it gets dark very early and on 22 December, lighting up time is usually about 4.15, with the light failing badly for about an hour before and if the weather is overcast, which it usually is at that time of the year, then it can be quite dark early in the afternoon. Consequently, if you are having a photographer to record your wedding it is really a better idea to get married about lunchtime in the winter, so that the photographer will be able to use the natural light.

In the Summer if you are late booking, you may find that it is impossible to have a 3 or 4 o'clock wedding in your local parish church, and even if you can, you will probably find that the best photographers, caterers, cars, are already booked for that time, so it is worth while making your preliminary enquiries as soon as possible.

LEGAL REQUIREMENTS

Before you can get married there are a few conditions which must be fulfilled. Firstly you must be over eighteen years of age (sixteen with parental consent) and secondly you must be free to marry. That is to say that if you have been married before you must have your decree absolute. Generally speaking, registry offices and churches which permit the marriage of divorced persons will not arrange a wedding on production of a decree nisi, let alone a pending divorce action. And, except for special licences as detailed below, you must have been resident in the appropriate district for twenty-one days. It is also necessary to take your birth certificates with you.

REGISTRY OFFICE WEDDINGS

The ceremony takes about ten minutes. The Bride and Groom enter the registry office together and the Registrar asks them to declare publicly that they 'know not of any reason' why they should not be joined in matrimony ('In public' means in front of a minimum of two other persons who act as witnesses). The couple then take one another as lawful man and wife. There is no promise ''til death us do part' and no religious overtones. It is a legal contract of marriage. Most Registry Offices are decked out with flowers and most Registrars wear suits, are smartly attired and make the ceremony very pleasant indeed. Frequently Brides wear white wedding dresses and nearly all carry flowers (see Appearance). Recently I saw a registry office Wedding where the Groom and Best Man wore Morning Dress. The one thing which is missing from a registry office ceremony is the music.

REGISTRAR'S CERTIFICATE

The Superintendent Registrar may issue a certificate with or without licence, all depending on the length of time which will elapse before the marriage takes place.

The only instance where a Registrar's certificate is not required is when the couple are to be married in the Church of England, but it must be obtained for all other denomination weddings.

SUPERINTENDENT REGISTRAR'S CERTIFICATE WITHOUT LICENCE

To qualify for this both the Bride and Groom must have lived in the area for at least seven days immediately prior to giving notice to the Registrar.

The notice can be given by either the Bride or the Groom, but if they live in different areas the notice has to be given to the Superintendent Registrars of each area.

The building in which the wedding is to take place must be stated in each notice of marriage.

At least twenty-one clear days must intervene between the day when the notice is entered in the Superintendent Registrar's notice book and the day when the Certificate is issued.

The marriage should then take place within three months of the Registrar's entry in his notice book.

SUPERINTENDENT REGISTRAR'S CERTIFICATE WITH LICENCE

This is the really 'high-speed' way of getting married. Both the Bride and Groom must be resident in England or Wales on the day the notice is entered in the notice book, but only one party need give the notice and only one of them need be resident in the registration district where the notice is given for fifteen days prior to the notice being given.

The marriage must take place in the building specified in the notice.

There need only be one clear day, not a Sunday, Christmas Day or Good Friday, between the notice and the issue of the certificate with licence.

Again the marriage should take place within three months of the entry of the notice. However, most people who apply for this kind of certificate are in a great hurry to get married and usually get married within a day or two.

CHURCH OF ENGLAND WEDDINGS

It is a tradition that weddings take place in the Bride's parish church, however, there is no law requiring this and the marriage can take place in the Groom's Parish Church or in one where the Bride and Groom have worshipped together for some time, making them eligible to be included in the Church's Electoral Roll.

If the Bride and Groom wish to get married in another church, then it is necessary for them or at least one of them to establish 'residence' in the Parish of that Church for a period of not less than 15 days prior to the wedding.

PUBLICATION OF BANNS

The word 'bann' means a proclamation. The banns were introduced in the fourteenth century by the presiding Archbishop of Canterbury as at that time a good deal of skulduggery was going on with marriages being organised for reason of finance or power, sometimes even between close relatives and sometimes bigamously, as there were no written records which could be referred to. Consequently marriages were required to take place during the hours of daylight and proclamations had to be read in appropriate districts, so that people could own up if they knew of a 'just cause or impediment' to the marriage and even today in marriage ceremonies there is still a pause for a last minute objection to be lodged. It was also at this time when the Laws of Consanguinity were introduced, which state that a man may not marry his grandmother or his brother's wife, and even today when a woman has lost her husband and wishes to marry his single brother, she must make application to the House of Lords for special permission.

A marriage in the Church of England can take place under several different types of notification. The simplest means and the most common is for the Bride and Groom to inform the Vicars in both parishes and the banns are read out in church on three consecutive Sundays in both parishes. At one time it was thought unlucky for the Bride and Groom to hear the banns being read, but today it is expected that they will attend church on at least one Sunday to hear their banns.

The Bride and Groom must be resident in the parishes in which the banns are read during the three weeks of their reading.

The vicar who performs the ceremony will require a certificate from the vicar of the other parish stating that the banns have been read.

If a period of three months is exceeded after the reading of the banns, then the banns have to be read again.

There is a fee payable for the publication of banns.

MARRIAGE BY COMMON LICENCE

This is the 'quicky' version, which short-circuits the need for the reading of the banns.

There are still residential requirements, but these only apply to one of the parties, who needs to have resided in the appropriate parish for fifteen days immediately before the application is made.

The licence may be granted by the Vicar himself, a nearby 'surrogate' whose address the Vicar will give, or by the Faculty Office. After the licence is issued the marriage may take place within three months, but usually again it takes place within a day or two.

The licence must be applied for in person and a fee is payable for this.

MARRIAGE BY SPECIAL LICENCE

This is applied for only in very special circumstances and is issued by the Archbishop of Canterbury through the Faculty Office, enabling a wedding to take place in any building, which may not be registered for marriage, e.g. hospital, etc. Fees are payable both to the Faculty Office and to the clergyman performing the ceremony.

DIVORCED PEOPLE

Generally speaking, the Church of England will not marry a couple where either partner has been divorced and the previous partner is still alive. However, there is a Service of Blessing which can be arranged and is very much like a wedding, except that the couple will have previously had a registry office wedding, where the actual legal part of the ceremony takes place. Sometimes this is done very quietly on the day before the church ceremony, or else on the same day with the church ceremony immediately following the civil one or one taking place in the morning and the other in the afternoon.

At a blessing it is normal for the Groom to accompany the Bride into the church and not her father and the Groom and Bride 'acknowledge' rather than 'take' each other as man and wife. Other than this, the ceremony is very similar to the standard marriage service.

ROMAN CATHOLIC WEDDINGS

It is normal to contact the Priest at least two to three months before the date of the intended marriage, as there are usually lessons which the couple receive from the Priest to prepare them for marriage.

The Priest will wish to see copies of both the Bride and Groom's baptism and Confirmation Certificates.

Whoever is not getting married in their own parish must obtain from their own Priest what is known as a 'Letter of Freedom', giving permission for the wedding to take place in another church.

The banns are only read when both the Bride and Groom are Catholics.

In the past only Catholics married Catholics, but today many Catholics are marrying out of the faith, but a Catholic still needs permission in the form of a special dispensation from a parish Priest in order to marry a non-Catholic.

If a Roman Catholic wishes to be married in another denomination church, then a dispensation is needed from a Bishop. Under these circumstances the Catholic partner has to agree to preserve their faith and the non-Catholic to respect the partner's faith and the Catholic partner has to agree to have the children baptized into the Catholic faith. The Priest will want to see the non-Catholic's Certificate of Baptism.

DIVORCE

The Roman Catholic Church does not approve of divorce and will not marry anyone who has been previously married whether they were married in the Roman Catholic religion or not.

NON-CONFORMIST RELIGIONS

The Baptist, Methodist and especially the United Reformed Church will marry people who have been divorced, but if the couple have been living together before marriage, some Ministers may refuse.

The ceremonies of the non-conformist religions are very similar to that of the Church of England, except that the Registrar is normally there for the signing of the register.

THE WEDDING RING

The wedding ring is probably the oldest surviving symbol of marriage. In fact early marriages were performed by the placing of a ring on the Bride's fourth finger of her left hand by the Groom in front of a Priest (because he was the most trustworthy person around) and that was all there was to it.

The word 'wedding' comes from the Anglo-Saxon word 'wed' meaning 'pledge' and the ring represented the pledge.

The ring is, by tradition, a plain band of gold. The plain un-interrupted circle represents eternity, and the gold, purity of intent. The reason the ring is placed on the fourth finger of the left hand is that the Romans erroneously believed that a vein called the Vena Amoris ran straight from it to the heart. Although this is not true, the tradition has continued.

At the time of Oliver Cromwell, rings were frowned upon as superstitious, but the Restoration of Charles II saw the re-introduction of rings in the wedding ceremony and their use has continued ever since.

The wedding ring should, by tradition be a plain band, although today many are patterned with a continuous design.

When selecting your wedding ring it might be a good idea to bear in mind that 18 carat gold and 22 carat gold wear very quickly and that the patterning will soon disappear. Also if you have a 9 carat gold engagement ring, which you intend to wear with your wedding ring, and if the wedding ring is 18 or 22 carat gold, then it will be softer than your engagement ring and the engagement ring will wear away the wedding ring. The higher the carat number, the purer the gold, the purer the gold, the softer the metal.

Also when trying on your wedding ring, think about the width. If it is very wide, then you may not be able to wear an eternity ring, which is traditionally given on the birth of the first child, as well as your engagement ring.

Wedding rings are usually bought from a jeweller's shop, although some people do buy them by post, especially as some 'Discount' jewellers now sell by post in order to get a larger turn-over of stock, enabling them to cut their costs. If buying by post, do make sure that you allow plenty of time for the ring to arrive and to allow for returning it and re-ordering if the fit is not good. Also if you are ordering by post and are choosing a wide ring, remember to order a couple of sizes larger than the ring sizer to be sure of being able to slip the ring over the knuckle.

If, for reasons of time or finance, a ring is not bought, it is quite legal to borrow one for the ceremony.

On the continent, the ring is worn on the fourth finger of the *right* hand.

It is considered very bad luck to drop the wedding ring on the wedding day, especially if its a Russian wedding ring, which is three loops of gold and was designed so that if the bride removed the ring from her hand in her husband's absence she could not put it back on again, she is, therefore, fraught with problems if it is dropped and she cannot find the secret of how it goes back together again.

WEDDING DAY SUPERSTITIONS

Something old, something new ...
Everyone knows the old adage

Something old, something new,
Something borrowed, something blue,

but there is a final line, which is little known and rarely quoted

'and a silver sixpence in your shoe'

The 'something old' represents the married woman's links with her family and her past and many Brides wear a piece of old jewellery, possibly an heirloom.

'Something new' represents that on her wedding day the Bride is starting a new life and looking forward to the future. Since most of the Bride's outfit is new most Brides feel that that is sufficient. However, if the Bride is, for example, wearing an heirloom necklace, then some Grooms like to send their Brides some new earrings, or a bracelet to wear on their wedding day, alternatively, the Bride's parents may decide to provide this small gift.

'Something borrowed' is to remind the Bride of how much we need to rely on the rest of the community to help us. Although Brides frequently 'borrow' something from their mothers, it is considered much more effective to borrow something from an aquaintance for example, their head-dress. However, the friend must then accept the loaned article back; to generously give it to her after the wedding does not enable her to fulfill the superstition.

'Something blue' is for faithfulness. Blue has always been the colour associated with faithfulness and the Bride, herself, must wear something which is blue, or has blue in it. Many Brides wear a garter, but if this is found to be uncomfortable, then a blue handkerchief may be secreted about the Bride's person. Or sometimes pale blue lace is introduced into the Bride's underwear.

'A silver sixpence in your shoe' is, these days more usually a five penny piece. The reason for this superstition is to wish the Bride wealth and financial comfort during her marriage.

Confetti
The throwing of confetti is a very watered down version of an ancient fertility rite, which used to take place at weddings.

Throughout history, all over the world Brides have had things thrown at them. In this country it used to be wheat, a symbol of fertility and good fortune. Also shoes used to be thrown at the bride, eventually the shoes, together with other symbols of love and marriage – hearts, flowers, bells, horseshoes, etc. combined with the wheat became small cakes. Confetti is the Italian word for confectionery, meaning the little iced cakes in the above shapes and now little pieces of coloured paper represent these cakes.

A confectioner who made these small cakes for illegal weddings which took place outside the Fleet prison is said to have had the idea of making a pile of cakes and icing over the top of them, and being inspired by the spire of nearby St. Bride's Church, made what is reputed to have been the first wedding cake.

In some areas the wheat which used to be thrown eventually was replaced by rice and rice is still thrown at many weddings today.

Also today many people throw computer punchings, which can be very unkind as they are extremely difficult to get rid of.

Garters

The garter that the Bride wears on her wedding day is believed to bring good luck. In the reign of Queen Victoria men would fight for them, or race on horseback from the church to the Bride's door to await the Bride's arrival and claim their prize.

Today, however, the Bride usually keeps her garter, but in some areas and in America, the Groom will actually remove the Bride's garter and when the Bride throws her bouquet to the unmarried girls, the Groom will throw the garter to the unmarried men.

Shoes and Horseshoes

Horseshoes are a very ancient symbol of fertility, as indeed are shoes, but to bring good luck the horseshoe must be stored upright, with the U shape pointing upwards 'to keep the luck in'.

Shoes are also a symbol of authority. At Anglo-Saxon weddings the Bride's father would give one of the Bride's shoes to the

Groom, who would then touch her on the head with it. Shoes feature in other wedding ceremonies in other parts of the world also.

At one time shoes were thrown at the newly married couple and it was considered very lucky, if rather painful, if a shoe hit them.

Today shoes are normally tied to the vehicle in which the Bride and Groom leave for their honeymoon. It is important that anyone taking on such a task makes sure that whatever he is tying the shoes to the vehicle with will break easily, so that it cannot become entwined in the mechanics of the car, or any other car, for that matter.

The Sweep

It has always been considered good luck to meet a sweep at a wedding, as he is closely associated with fire and warmth and the hearth and home. The sweep must be covered in soot and carrying his brushes and the Bride and Groom must speak to him and shake hands with him. It is reported that on his wedding day, Prince Philip saw a sweep passing by as he was preparing to leave for his wedding and went down and spoke to him. Ideally, the sweep should be invited to walk a short distance with the whole wedding party, but it is a nice gesture, if a sweep comes to the wedding, to invite him back either for a drink or even some food.

Mirrors

It is considered good luck for the Bride to glance in her mirror, just once before leaving for her wedding, when fully attired and it is for this reason that the photographer likes the Bride to be ready and waiting for him in her bedroom, so that he can take a photograph of her looking into the mirror before she has her other photographs taken. It is considered bad luck to return to look in the mirror after she has left the bedroom as she has then commenced her journey to her wedding. There are many superstitions about returning once a journey has commenced and this is but one of them.

CHURCH AND HALL COSTS

Ceremony

Church/Registry Office	£
Licence	£
Choir	£
Organist	£
Bells	£
Church Flowers	£

1. Name _____   Price per hour   £
   Address _____   Kitchen hire   £
   Tel: _____   Extras   £
   Contact _____   VAT   £
   Max. No. of People _____   Total   £ _____

2. Name _____   Price per hour   £
   Address _____   Kitchen hire   £
   Tel: _____   Extras   £
   Contact _____   VAT   £
   Max No. of People _____   Total   £ _____

3. Name _____   Price per hour   £
   Address _____   Kitchen hire   £
   Tel: _____   Extras   £
   Contact _____   VAT   £
   Max. No. of People _____   Total   £ _____

Hall decided on _____ Total Cost   £

Deposit paid £ _____ Balance of £ _____ on

_____ (date)

TOTAL   £ _____

Naming the Day

ESTIMATE

Item	Total cost	Deposit Paid	Blance Due	Date Due
Church				
Licence				
Hall				
Stationery				
Photographer				
Cars				
Flowers				
Cake				
Catering				
Appearance				
Honeymoon				
Contingency Fund				
Total £				

The Photographer

WHY A PROFESSIONAL

This is the only part of a wedding where we do strongly recommend that you hire a professional. It must be borne in mind that when the whole day is over and your new life begins, the only thing you will have to remind you of this very special occasion, is your photographs. If you economise too greatly on this aspect of your wedding, then you will, without doubt, regret it later. Some people think that an uncle with a good camera who takes 'nice' photographs, is qualified to take their wedding photographs, and this will help to cut their expenses, but in spite of an expensive camera, uncle is unlikely to have spent a tenth of that which the professional has spent on his equipment. The materials used by amateurs, especially the film, are also likely to be different. But the most important thing to bear in mind is experience.

The professional will know what to do if the weather is bad, if the light is bad. Amateurs are inclined to use a flash gun to give them light if a summer sky suddenly becomes stormy and overcast, and this will make the photographs look as though they were taken at midnight.

Taking a family group photograph takes years of experience

44

to obtain good results, as do taking soft focus shots and other special effects.

It is doubtful whether an amateur could arrange for super-imposed photographs to be done for you, such as the Bride and Groom superimposed on a music sheet, or a brandy glass. Remember the professional photographer's reputation is at stake every time he photographs a wedding and if he is a well known local photographer he will be well aware of this and, therefore, extremely conscientious when taking your wedding photographs.

The trouble with allowing an amateur to take the photographs is that if they do not turn out well there will be no opportunity to take more photographs and the record of your wedding is lost for ever.

CHOOSING A PROFESSIONAL

A lot of people seem to ring round for prices from photographers and this seems to me to be a very silly idea. It is rather like telephoning dress shops to find out how much their dresses are. Some shops sell dresses priced from £10.00, some from £100. You would expect the shop selling the most expensive dresses to stock the best and it probably will. With photographers it is much the same sort of thing. With your dress, before setting out to buy, you will probably have an idea of the style you would like, but it is unlikely that you will have looked around various photographers to see which different styles they offer.

There are other things to bear in mind as well; how long has the photographer been established and is he qualified? These are not guarantees of quality, but they are a guide. If a photographer belongs to one of the professional associations, then this means that he has to conform to a code of practice and if you feel that you have been badly treated by him, then you can refer to his association. When making enquiries, it is a good idea to make a note of the association to which he belongs, as it is easier to find this out at the beginning, rather than later, if you do have problems, however unlikely this may be.

If the photographer holds a qualification at one of the professional associations, then this signifies that he has reached a high standard of proficiency.

VAT registration is something else to look for. Although this is absolutely no guarantee of quality, it does mean that the photographer achieves a fairly high turnover, which means he must be gaining experience in his field.

Recommendation is the most popular method of people finding a photographer, but do not just ask someone else who has just got married who photographed their wedding, but delve more deeply and find out whether they were really satisfied with the result. Find out why they did not buy copies of the remaining photographs, especially if they have a particularly thin wedding album. Also remember, if you are asking someone who has been married a year or two that businesses do change hands.

Beware of photographers who seem to be a lot cheaper than other local photographers. Generally speaking, these are people who work during the week, and are really not a lot better than keen amateurs as they will not be getting the experience of full time professional photography.

Beware of free offers, this can mean that these particular photographers are not getting enough work, and although you may get something free, your photographs may be disappointing. Also if you are tempted by a 'free offer' make sure that it is 'free', by asking how much the photographs would normally cost.

Beware of recommendations from other people in the 'wedding business'. Frequently this is not because they think that a particular photographer is better than any other, but because the photographer pays them a commission, which means that, although you should not refuse to see such people, you should look very carefully at what they are offering and make sure that you are getting what you pay for.

AMATEUR PHOTOGRAPHERS

As stated above, a friend who will provide photos for what it costs him or someone who will do it for nothing, or as a wedding present, we do not think is a very good idea, because if it all goes wrong, not only have you lost your wedding photographs, but you may have lost a valued friend or relative.

SEMI-PROFESSIONALS

Semi-professionals are photographers who work at another job during the week and, therefore, fall between being professional and amateur. In other parts of the E.E.C. or Common Market, this is illegal, but as most weddings take place on a Saturday, it is a popular form of 'moonlighting'. These photographers cannot usually be contacted by telephone during the week, or advertise their telephone number as 'after six'. Not only do they lack professional experience and expertise, but they can also be annoyingly inaccessible when queries arise. They do not rely on their ability and reputation to earn their living as they have another job.

Subcontractors
This is where a caterer, for example, asks if you would like to see 'our photographer'. He may either work under their name or under his own. It is important to establish who he is and who has legal responsibility for his work, as this is another way in which you may find yourself with another semi-professional, so do compare his prices and work with other local photographers. Whenever you see a photographer, do ask whether he actually took those photographs or if the photographer who is going to take your photographs took them.

Operators
Operators are a very sticky problem. A lot of photographers use them. They may be trained amateurs, untrained amateurs, other

professionals who have no work on your particular wedding day (some professionals have this arrangement) or even someone equally as untrained as 'uncle'. It is therefore important to establish when booking your wedding photographer exactly who will be taking your wedding photographs, his name (or her name), his experience and to make sure that you have seen some of his work.

Salesmen with a different man on the day

There are photographic businesses who actually send out professional salesmen, who use 'hard sell' techniques to get you to book with them and it is with these sort of people you are most likely to get an untrained operator who has never or rarely photographed a wedding before. The best way of ensuring that you do not get one of these companies is to make sure that you book with a Company who is registered with either the Master Photographers Association or the British Institute of Professional Photographers, or better still, is qualified with them.

WHEN AND WHERE PHOTOGRAPHS ARE TAKEN

It is only possible to give a guide as to what photographs a photographer will take, as different photographers approach the subject from a different angle.

At Home

Not all wedding photographers take photographs of the Bride at home and when making enquiries, if you do definitely require photographs to be taken before you leave for the church, it is worth enquiring whether he does this as a matter of course or whether there would be an extra charge. I always feel that the best photographs are taken at home of the Bride.

In the bedroom, the photographer may take a close up or two of the Bride, and maybe the Bride with her mother adjusting the veil and handing her daughter her bouquet.

In the sitting room he may take pictures of the Bride seated on her own, with her Bridesmaids and perhaps with her parents. It is necessary to ensure that the room is empty of people and in a very tidy condition. The photographer will be looking for a plain and simple background to seat the bride against, like curtains for example, and may wish to move the furniture around to achieve the best effect.

In fine weather the photographer will probably want to take the Bride and her Bridesmaids into the garden to take some photographs there, especially if there is a nice garden, in which case he may dispense with those in the sitting room or use both. If you do not have a very good garden, then why not ask a neighbour if you can use theirs. A good garden to a photographer is not one where there is necessarily a lot of flowers. It is a garden where there are plenty of trees, which cut out confusing background, such as roofs of houses, washing lines, sheds and greenhouses, especially when in a state of decay.

At The Church

BEFORE THE CEREMONY

Most professional photographers pose the Bride and her father, or whoever is giving her away at the door of the house, before they leave to get to the church in advance of the other members of the wedding party. When the photographer arrives at the church approximately twenty minutes before the appointed hour of the ceremony, he will normally look for the Groom and Best Man and take a couple of photographs of them together, shaking hands, or the Best Man adjusting the Groom's buttonhole. After this the Groom and Best Man are then free to enter the church to see the Vicar and take their seats.

The photographer will then await the arrival of the Bridesmaids together with the Bride's mother and photograph them either leaving the car or in the doorway of the church. This should happen about ten minutes before the arrival of the Bride. The Bridesmaids wait in the doorway of the church for the Bride and the Bride's mother with the Ushers making sure that everyone is seated in church, including all amateur photographers, before the Bride enters the church.

At this moment it is not usually considered a good idea to take photographs because it could make the service late to commence, which is unfair if there is another wedding to follow.

DURING THE CEREMONY

Photographs being taken during the ceremony are always a thorny problem. The Roman Catholic Church and Non-Conformist religions usually permit at least some photographs to be taken. With the Church of England it varies considerably, all depending on the Vicar concerned. Some permit anything to be taken, with flash guns, some without. Most do not permit photographs to be taken during prayers, especially with the flash gun. Some will allow one or two shots from the back without the use of the flash. Bearing in mind that when the photographer is not allowed to use his flash gun and the light levels are quite low, then it is very difficult to get 'action' shots as these tend to appear blurred when processed.

It is also worth thinking about just how many photographs you will want to buy of the ceremony. The photographer will not be able to pose the Bride and Groom or any of the guests, to ensure that he gets the best possible photograph of everyone, and even when he is allowed to go up to the front to photograph the exchange of rings, he will probably only be able to take this from the side, which normally involves getting only the sides or even backs of the Bride and Groom's head and I always feel that one good photograph taken from the back of the church, with more photographs later is a better solution. However, if one of your friends has had a particularly nice photograph taken in the church and you would like a similar one, ask her if you can borrow her album to show to the photographer when giving your final instructions to him shortly before the wedding.

Some Vicars like the Bride and Groom to complete the legal formalities, i.e. signing the register, in the middle of the ceremony and some at the end. Wherever this takes place, the photographer always comes forward to photograph the Bride and Groom signing the register. What normally happens is that the Bride and Groom and the two witnesses complete the signing and then the Vicar replaces one of the Registers and a posed photograph is taken. A photograph of the Vicar handing the marriage licence to the couple can be taken, if the Vicar is amenable to this idea.

Some of the most important photographs of any wedding are those taken when the Bride and Groom come down the aisle and it can be expected that all photographers will take at least two pictures at this time, and then perhaps one of the Bride and Groom as they go through the church door, with their faces turned looking back into church. It is a good idea to ask the Vicar how he feels about photographs being taken in his church and to make sure that any guests bringing cameras with them are aware of his requirements. Even those Vicars who allow photography in church can get quite upset if, when the photographer goes forward to take the 'signing' pictures, he is accompanied by a number of guests, who proceed to spend ten minutes or more taking pictures. Some vicars have been known to stop the service and threaten not to continue until cameras are put away. This can be very embarrassing and to prevent this it is better to speak to your guests in advance, requesting them not to take photos during the ceremony. Also when coming down the aisle, if someone fires a flash gun at the same time as the photographer, then the photograph which you have paid for can be ruined.

OUTSIDE THE CHURCH
Here again is where the Bride and Groom and their parents, the best man and the Ushers can help the photographer to take much better pictures. Very few people like to work with other people looking over their shoulder and photographers are no exception to this. It is very inconvenient to have people standing behind you when taking photographs. For one thing it is possible to step back on them, especially children, and hurt them. Also it means that in all their photographs the photographer's back will be in them. Apart from this, when the photographer is taking a picture

and he wants the Bride and Groom to look at the camera, if some-one calls to them and they look away, or, worse still, one of them looks away, then the picture is ruined.

Our solution to this is to give the guests, say, five minutes during which they can take as many pictures as they would like and pose the Bride and Groom as they would like, after which time they are asked to stand a long way back, just so that they can hear when the photographer calls them to come into a group photo-graph. There is then, obviously no reason for them not to come into the group, since they should have taken all the photographs that they want. It is usual to take about five group photographs.

Following the group photographs, we will take the Bride and Groom away and take five or six 'romantic' shots of them on their own. The poses for these are a matter of individual taste and flair, but, again, if there is one particular type of pose which you favour, for example, sitting down on the grass, then do tell the photographer, or show him your friend's photograph which you particularly liked.

After all this is done it is normal for the photographer to ask the guests to throw their confetti and to take photographs of this. Many churches request that confetti is not thrown in the grounds, and the photographer will then ask the guests to do this in the street, which is in actual fact 'Littering' and liable to a fine of £10, but I have never known anyone to be fined yet.

After the throwing of the confetti, the Bride and Groom then go to the car and may have a couple of photographs taken in or outside of the car.

AT THE RECEPTION

Obviously the cutting-of-the-cake pictures are most important. If you require a picture of the cake on its own, make sure that your photographer realises this. Normally there are photographs taken of the Bride and Groom with glasses toasting one another. Also if you have elderly or invalid guests, then it is better to take pictures of them at the reception, rather than at the church.

Normally the guests are not let into the reception until the photographer has finished his work and gone and the Bride and Groom are free to greet their guests, although sometimes this is overlooked where the weather is unpleasant and guests need to be hurried indoors.

How Many and How Long

Most photographers ask the Bride to be ready for them one hour before the time of the ceremony, but some will ask for up to one and a half hours. Obviously more time is required if there is a long journey to the church. At this stage it is usual to take between ten and fifteen photographs.

At the church and after the ceremony, approximately twenty to thirty photographs are taken over a period of twenty to forty minutes, the ceremony taking twenty minutes to half an hour, although some ceremonies are longer, especially Roman Catholic ones, when mass is said.

At the reception the photographer usually takes between five and ten photographs, taking another ten minutes.

The average wedding album contains thirty-five to forty photographs, although some have sixty and a few thirty, although we feel that thirty and less does not give a full coverage of the day's events and makes the album look rather thin.

Helping your photographer

The first and most important thing is to be on time. There is nothing worse for a photographer than for him to turn up at the appointed hour to find the Bride with curlers still in her hair, and not dressed. Make all hairdressing appointments early in the morning, even if the hairdresser is coming to the house. Do not try to make it an 'after lunch rush', as you would when, say, going to a dinner party. For a 3 p.m. wedding, ideally the Bride and Bridesmaids should all be ready, bar, perhaps their lipstick and clothes, by the time they eat lunch.

When leaving for the church, make sure that the car hire company are informed of how long it takes to get to the church on a busy Saturday afternoon. And let the caterers know that you will be arriving an hour and a quarter to an hour and a half after the time of the ceremony, so that you do not have to worry about the food spoiling and there is adequate time for the photographer to create whatever effect he wants without having to rush.

The Bride and Groom are also in the best position to control the guests as far as getting them into groups is concerned, and stopping them taking photographs when the photographer has asked them not to. Some photographers will refuse to work whilst guests are taking pictures. If you put it to your guests that what you would like them to do is to take the pictures the photographer will not take, then this will avoid giving offence. These can be of guests standing in groups chatting, what young Bridesmaids get up to whilst they are not in front of the professional camera, and even more important, when the photographer has gone, to photograph the actual cutting of the cake, the speeches and the dancing and celebrations in the evening, rather than to copy every single photograph which the photographer takes.

Checking Your Booking

Your photographer will probably ask you to pay him a fortnight or so before the wedding although this is by no means the rule, some make it a month and others on the day, but if you do not receive any communication by about a fortnight before the wedding, it is a good idea to telephone to clear this point. You should also contact your photographer on the day before your wedding to make sure that he has you in mind.

When you telephone him, check all the details with him to make sure that nothing has changed, especially the date and time, the church, the Bride's address, the reception, etc. These are details he should have taken in the beginning, but things do change and notes get lost, so do check. Find out what time he plans to arrive.

If the Photographer does not arrive

If no one turns up at the appointed time, give him only five minutes and *ring*. If you still cannot be sure that he is on his way, start ringing round other photographers in the area. You should still have your list from when you went to see all the prospective photographers. Find out if there is anyone who could possibly meet you at the church. If he is half an hour late, then get another photographer to meet you at the church. Point out what has happened and see if he will agree a fee to be paid to him if the other photographer turns up. If, however, your photographer is so late that you have booked another one, you are probably within your rights to send the first one away, although problems arise if you have already paid him for your photographs and album. If you have selected a photographer as described earlier, this sort of situation would only occur under very severe circumstances, such as a motor accident. If you have booked a good local photographer and he does not turn up to take your photographs you can be sure that he will refund your money. A second photographer taking on the job, though, may also want some money in advance, and this is why it is good to have a 'contingency fund', so that you can write a cheque or give a credit card number, but remember, not all photographers take credit cards, so you may have to raise the cash.

Contractual Liability

Some photographers charge an attendance fee, which is a fee they charge just to photograph the wedding. That is to say that the pictures are taken onto film. Most photographers who charge this, take this as a booking fee; others will add this amount to the cost of the number of photographs (sometimes their minimum number, sometimes the number of photographs you say you will want to buy) and the cost of the album and then, say, ask for a 25% deposit. It varies. If it is a 25% deposit, then you can expect this amount to be deducted from the end price, but if it is an attendance fee, then this is not deductable.

If you have only paid an attendance fee the photographer will turn up at your wedding even if you do not pay the balance, but he will not have the photographs processed, so you will not be able to see what pictures he has taken but the Attendance Fee does guarantee that you will have a photographer.

If you cancel your wedding, or decide to use another photographer, you cannot expect to have your money refunded. In fact, the photographer may ask you to pay a percentage of the amount he would have charged you, all depending on how close to the date of the wedding the cancellation comes. If for some reason the wedding has to be postponed, most photographers will transfer a deposit or attendance fee to that date, although they are not obliged to do so.

When passing orders for photographs to a photographer, it is best to put these in writing, as a photographer will not correct any errors, unless he has written evidence that it was his fault.

The photographer has the copyright to all the poses which he sets up and can sue anyone 'covering' his photographs.

Certain fabrics in certain lighting conditions can be difficult to get right in colour photographs. The colours in a colour photograph are balanced to skin tones and to make sure that the Bride's dress is white (if she is wearing a white dress) if then other colours do not look right, this is referred to as anomalous reflectance. It occurs with a few man–made fabrics in certain colours.

Sometimes, in the spring and autumn, the sunlight making an oblique angle with the earth causes the photographs to have a 'golden glow'. I always think that this is rather attractive and I have never known anyone to complain about it.

After a certain time some photographers charge a little extra above the cost of their photographs for locating old negatives. Some photographers also add on a handling charge for a small order of, say, one photograph.

When they hand you the proofs, most photographers will indicate a time limit when they expect to receive instructions for prints required. The previews and proofs always remain the property of the photographer.

If you are not satisfied

If you are not satisfied with your photographs, or the amount of money you have been charged, if the photographer is a member of one of the professional associations, then you can ask them to mediate on your behalf. They do this on a strictly impersonal basis. It is therefore a very good idea to make sure that your photographer belongs to one of these associations, but if he does not then your only hope is to contact the Trading Standards Officer, but he will only be interested in really serious cases (i.e. where there were no photographs) and offers nothing like the protection of a professional association.

VIDEOS

The main advantage of a video is that it gives an account of the wedding as it happens, recording every detail and can record the wedding service, words and pictures and the music as well. It should be noted that if you record the wording of the marriage service and/or music which is still in copyright, permission should be sought and a fee is usually payable to the publisher or to the copyright holder.

A video film is very expensive to make usually costing more than the average wedding album, all depending on what you have filmed. Obviously the most important parts are the church service and the reception. Before booking a video, it is important to check with the Minister to make sure that he has no objections to the film being taken and the lighting being set up in his church. There is nothing worse than paying hundreds for a video to be done and to find when the cameraman turns up at the church with his engineer that there are restrictions preventing him from setting up lighting or filming in church. If you are not allowed to film in church, then we feel that a video is pointless. At the reception it is good to have the speeches filmed, provided those giving speeches feel happy about it. Most Brides also feel the need for still photographs, so that they can carry them to work, etc. and show to people who do not have video machines.

Also it is possible that video machines will change in the fairly near future, making the film obsolete. The films also have a more limited life than still photographs. Very few Brides and Grooms have video machines themselves anyway.

The most important thing to remember is that for still photographs you only have a few minutes training to become a model. For a video you have to act as well!

PHOTOGRAPHY

Photographer 1

Attendance Fee	£
Photographs (size ___)	£
Album (name _____)	£
Special Effects	£
VAT	£

Marks out of ten for quality ——

Name _____
Address _____
Tel _____
Qualifications _____

Photographer 2

Attendance Fee	£
Photographs (size ___)	£
Album (name _____)	£
Special Effects	£
VAT	£

Marks out of ten for quality ___

Name _____
Address _____
Tel _____
Qualifications _____

Photographer 3

Attendance Fee	£
Photographs (size ___)	£
Album (name _____)	£
Special Effects	£
VAT	£

Marks out of ten for quality ___

Name _____
Address _____
Tel _____
Qualifications _____

Photographer 4

Attendance Fee	£
Photographs (size ___)	£
Album (name _____)	£
Special Effects	£
VAT	£

Marks out of ten for quality ___

Name _____
Address _____
Tel _____
Qualifications _____

Photographer selected_____

Attendance fee/deposit paid £_____.   Balance of £_____ due on _____ (date).

Stationery

Printed invitations are well worth investing in. A simple single card with the invitation printed on it is all that is needed, rather than the more expensive book style invitations and this will only cost a couple of pounds more than buying ready made invitations which have to be written in. It is a very arduous task to write all the details of a wedding into twenty invitations, if this increases, then the task becomes Herculean.

Many people who supply other things you may book for your wedding will probably supply stationery, namely photographers and wedding dress shops, but the more obvious suppliers are stationers and card shops. The unprinted type, where you have to write the details in yourself are usually only found in card shops, and occasionally in stationers.

WEDDING INVITATIONS

Ordering
Generally speaking, wedding invitations take about a fortnight to come from the date of order, although they can take longer.

If a mistake is made in the printing, then it can obviously take a further two to three weeks to sort it out, so in order to be on the safe side, it is preferable to think about ordering the stationery once the church and reception have been booked. Bear in mind that once you have looked at the stationery you may decide that you want your mother to look at what you have chosen, or your fiance and this can take time to organise.

Remember that you do not have to send out your invitations immediately you get them, but if you get them late, then you could face problems and even panic.

The latest you should order stationery is three months before the date of the wedding. Of course, if you plan to marry at short notice, then it is possible to order them up to two months before the wedding.

Sending them out

Some people say that wedding invitations should be sent out six weeks before the date of the wedding, but really, this is rather late these days, two to three months is more usual.

When marrying in the summer, it is important that people know well in advance when your wedding is so that they can arrange their holidays accordingly, especially members of the family and close friends. Immediately you have booked the church and reception, even if it is a year in advance, it is a good idea to sit down and work out a rough guest list, so that you can let those people who are the most important know when your wedding is when you see them, and then order your invitations, so that you can send them out about three months before the wedding.

Wording Invitations

Assuming that the Bride's parents are arranging everything, or most of the wedding and that the Bride is still living either with her parents or fairly close by, then the wording of the invitations can be as follows.

This one is the most usual and the most formal:

MR AND MRS J SMITH
request the pleasure of the company of
. . . .
at the marriage of their daughter
ELIZABETH
with
MR ALAN JONES
at All Saints Church, London
on Saturday, 1st August, 1984
at 3 p.m.
and afterwards at
The Railway Hotel, London.

5 Maytree Walk,
Evenstone,
London.   RSVP

A slightly less formal method of wording an invitation, without the necessity of writing in the name of the guest(s) is as follows:

MR & MRS J SMITH

would like you to join them
to celebrate the marriage of their daughter

ELIZABETH
and
MR ALAN JONES

at All Saints Church, Evenstone
on Saturday, 1st August, 1984
at 3 p.m.
The Reception afterwards will be held at
The Railway Hotel, Evenstone

Please reply to
5 Maytree Walk,
Evenstone,
Kent.

DIVORCED PARENTS AND WIDOWS
If either of the above wordings are required where the parents are divorced, then both names should be used (if the mother is remarried, then her new name is used) for example if Mr and Mrs Smith were divorced and Mrs Smith had remarried Mr Carl Brown, her own christian name being Mary, then the beginning of the invitation would read:

MR JOHN SMITH & MRS C. BROWN
request the pleasure, etc.

If, however, Mrs Smith's husband had died and she has not re-married then the invitation would read:

MRS MARY SMITH
requests the pleasure, etc.

However, if Mrs Smith has remarried since her husband's death, then the invitation would read:

MRS C. BROWN (or if everyone is agreeable MR AND MRS C. BROWN)
request the pleasure, etc. ...
at the marriage of her/their daughter (especially if Mr Brown has brought her up)
ELIZABETH SMITH

However, if this sort of complication needs to be avoided then the following wording can be used

Dear ....
would you please come to the wedding of our daughter
ELIZABETH
and
MR ALAN JONES
at All Saints Church, Evenstone
on Saturday, 1 August, 1984
at 3 p.m.
There will be a Reception afterwards
at The Railway Hotel, Evenstone.

Mr and Mrs C. Brown
5 Maytree Walk,
Evenstone,
Kent.   RSVP

Again, the joint names should be used where divorced parents are jointly arranging their daughter's wedding, but it does not look so obvious if just the mother's name is used.

If a brother and sister-in-law are arranging the wedding, or some other relatives, maybe grandparents, then those relationships are mentioned in the invitations:

Mr and Mrs F. Smith
request the pleasure, etc.
to the marriage of their sister

or a grandmother would write

Mrs T. Smith
requests the pleasure, etc.
at the marriage of her granddaughter.

Sending the invitations yourself

Where it is a second marriage, or where the Bride and Groom are already living together, especially in another area, where it is more convenient to arrange the wedding, then there are two wordings using the 'passive voice', which does not say who is inviting the guest, just that they are invited. The Bride would probably use her own address for the reply in these instances, although where parental complications make it difficult to word an invitation, then the first alternative can be used.

Brideshouse,
7 Colton Street,
Hadleigh Borough,
Essex.

ELIZABETH SMITH & ALAN JONES
would be pleased if you would
attend their wedding
on Saturday, 1 August, 1984
at All Saints Church,
Petherstone Road, Hadleigh Borough

The service commences at 3 p.m.
and will be followed by a reception
at the White Horse Inn, Hadleigh Vale,
Essex.
RSVP

The next version gives the guest a better idea of who is arranging the wedding:

ELIZABETH AND ALAN
are to be married at
All Saints Church,
Petherstone Road, Hadleigh Borough

on Saturday, 1 August, 1984
at 3 p.m.

and request the pleasure of your company.

The service will be followed by a reception
at the White Horse Inn, Hadleigh Vale, Essex.

Miss E. Smith,
Brideshouse,
7 Colton Street,
Hadleigh Borough,
Essex.

The Bride who wishes to send a very personal invitation, perhaps to a rather informal affair could use this wording, more in the form of a letter

Dear ...
Would you please come to my wedding to
ALAN JONES.
We are to be married
at Hadleigh Registry Office
Petherstone Road, Hadleigh Borough
on Friday, 31 July, 1984
at 3 p.m.
and are holding a reception afterwards
at The White Horse Inn, Hadleigh Vale

Yours sincerely,
(signed Elizabeth)

Miss E. Smith,
Brideshouse,
7 Colton Street,
Hadleigh Borough,
Essex.   RSVP

MAPS

At most weddings some of the guests come from a long way away and may not, therefore, know the area. It is also remarkable to note just how few people actually know their own locality, especially if the church, say, is off the beaten track, so it is a good idea to copy a map, showing the whereabouts of the church, the reception, the local railway station, taxi ranks, bus stops, etc. Then you can have this photostatted. Sometimes employers, if asked nicely, will agree to you doing this at work and, maybe, make a nominal charge for it. If this is not possible then go to a copyshop, or some stationers and public libraries provide this service. If it is rather expensive it may be better to copy the map two or three times onto one piece of paper – find out what size paper the machines takes first.

WEDDING LISTS

This is the time also to copy your wedding present list, keeping a master copy, so that when people return the list to you you can mark off what people have committed themselves to buying for you and if you get a duplication you can ring the person concerned and let them know. For this reason it is important to ask people to return the wedding list when they have made their decision.

RECEPTION INVITATIONS

Today one fashion is for the family and close friends to be invited to the wedding ceremony and for a 'wedding breakfast' to be held immediately afterwards and then for there to be a 'disco' with a finger buffet and drinks in the evening. In this case some people send out separate 'Reception Invitations'. These may be the handwritten type or printed. If printed, the wording will follow the form below:

MR & MRS J. SMITH
request the pleasure of the company of
....
at an Evening Reception
to celebrate the marriage of their daughter

ELIZABETH
with
MR ALAN JONES

to be held at
The Railway Hotel, Evenstone
on Saturday 1 August, 1984
at 7.30 p.m.
5 Maytree Walk
Evenstone, Kent.   RSVP

Obviously, this wording can be varied as the earlier examples given, depending on who is sending the invitation.

Quantities
To work out how many invitations you want, you must make

a list of all those *families* you intend to invite, together with couples, and single people.

Where a family have a grown up son, who has a girlfriend, it is then customary to send one invitation to the parents and any young children and another to the older son and his girlfriend. If inviting a single person then it is also customary to invite John Smith and friend. The same applies to people who may be separated or divorced, unless you are inviting their other partner. If the other partner is invited, then it is a kindness to mention this to them as they may not wish to come, especially if the separation is recent and feelings are acrimonious.

Having arrived at a rough figure add ten invitations for those you have forgotten, unless you are really limited with numbers. Or for people you have not invited, but would like to invite, in case someone sends a regret and then you can invite them without the embarrassment of having to say you have run out of invitations, which makes it seem like an afterthought.

Then add another five, for the ones that you might make a mistake on, plus a couple to keep, especially for your mum and yourself as these are the people who do not receive invitations, but are the most likely people to want one for sentimental reasons.

Most printers will print a minimum number of twenty and then increase in tens, so always round up, never down. If you find you have ordered too few, you cannot order another ten, you have to have twenty, when ten more ordered with your original invitations would only cost a couple of pounds extra, but a re-order of twenty could easily cost ten times that amount.

REPLIES

When you make the guest list, keep it. This is important, so that as you get the replies you can mark them off. It is amazing the number of people who think they do not have to reply to a wedding invitation. Some people think that if they do not reply the hosts will think they are not coming, others assume that if they do not reply, the hosts will assume that they are coming.

Ideally you want all the replies by three to four weeks before the wedding. However, probably by the week four stage, you will find that quite a few people have not replied and it will be necessary to ring round in order to have some idea of numbers. Some guests may also reply, however wrong this may be, by telephone and by keeping the list, you will be able to mark them off either as acceptances or regrets.

ORDERS OF SERVICE

The orders of service provide a guide to the wedding service, and do give the words of the hymns, but they do not give the exact words of the wedding service. Basically they are unnecessary, especially if you are trying to save money, as the church will supply hymn books and a copy of the service for guests to follow. They are very expensive, usually more expensive than the invitations and you will need to order more as one is required for each guest.

Dealing with the Minister

It is important that, if you wish to use Orders of Service, the minister performing the ceremony is aware of this and you should talk to him before ordering these. You also need to know if he is giving an address and if so when. You will need to know how many hymns and which ones before ordering as well. Also the Groom needs to remind the Minister on the day of the wedding that you are using Orders of Service and to make sure that he has a copy.

When to order

Again, these should be ordered well in advance, so that any mistakes can be rectified. Although these only need to be available a day before the wedding, so a month before should be the latest they are ordered. However they could be ordered as late as three weeks prior to the wedding.

Quantities

As stated above, at least one per person is required, but, again, you must allow at least ten spares. It is normal at most weddings for friends and neighbours who may not have been invited to the church to come along to see the Bride and it can be very embarrassing if, as the last guests filter in, there are not sufficient Orders of Service to go round. The Minister will not have arranged for hymn books to be laid out and will not announce the numbers of the hymns once he has been informed that there are Orders of Service.

It is also customary to supply a copy for each member of the choir. The Bride and Groom will also require one each, as will the Bridesmaids and arrangements should be made to make sure that the Bridesmaids have them, by getting the people who sit at the aisle ends of the pews to hold copies to give to them. The Groom should take two copies with him, one for him and one for the Bride. The Best Man can hold onto these. You may also require one to keep with your wedding album, and one each for each of the mothers in case theirs gets lost or misplaced on the wedding day. It is also a nice idea to send one to anyone who cannot get to the service, especially through illness, together with their piece of the wedding cake, and perhaps a wedding photograph, especially grandparents.

Serviettes

PERSONALISED SERVIETTES

Personalised serviettes are less common these days. If the personalised type are used, these are usually kept to wrap the wedding cake in.

NAPKIN RINGS

Napkin rings which are personalised are becoming much more popular. They are made of stiff paper with a pretty pattern on them, usually matching other table stationery, especially the place cards and can usually be supplied with coloured napkins to match your colour scheme.

PLAIN SERVIETTES

Both the personalised serviettes and the napkin rings are an unnecessary expense, especially if you are on a tight budget, and quite often a more striking effect can be obtained by using plain coloured serviettes, which are extremely economically priced and serve exactly the same function. If you use your colour scheme to full effect, with, say bridesmaids in pink, pink flowers, pink decoration on the cake and pink serviettes neatly folded standing in wine glasses, then you need little skill or money to achieve a very striking effect.

Coloured napkins are usually readily available at most stationery suppliers, newsagents and card shops. However, if you can only get white ones then it is possible to fold these in a very attractive fashion and if you like to decorate them with a paper tissue 'carnation' to emphasise your colour scheme.

PLACE CARDS

Place cards are absolutely essential. A good table plan, which shows everyone where they should sit, enables guests to relax and saves them the worry of searching for a place. Also without a table plan everyone sits down where they want to, family groups sitting together and this often means that people who get lost on their way back from the church or are late for some reason get separated when they sit down, there being two places at one table and one at another, if there are, say, three members of a family. So for a relaxed atmosphere, place cards and a table plan may take a little time to organize, but the cost will be nominal and they will make your guests feel cared for and leave a lasting impression.

Place cards can be obtained from the same shops which sell other items of stationery and can be personalised, although this tends to make them very expensive. They can be purchased to match napkin rings, although these also tend to be quite pricey. Place cards can also be bought 'off the peg', like the invitations which you write in yourself and these are relatively cheap and a search may enable you to buy something that will fit in with your colour scheme.

Failing this, the cheapest place cards can be made up out of plain white or coloured card, especially if you have the use of a guillotine. Even pieces of paper can be used. If you are artistic then you could draw a small simple design on these and paint them, if you have the time, say, two hearts, or bells, or a little flower.

HOW TO WRITE THEM

When writing out the cards it is not really good enough just to put christian names. The names should be written out in full, and it works like this: assuming that there is a family of four called Smith the husband's name is John, the wife is Mary, the daughter is Elizabeth and the son Daniel. Mr Smith's card is written as Mr J. Smith or Mr John Smith. Mrs Smith's card is written as Mrs J. Smith or Mrs John Smith. The daughter's card is written as Miss Elizabeth Smith and the son's card as Master Daniel Smith. If he is quite grown up he could be called Daniel Smith, but once fully grown, say sixteen he should be referred to as Mr Daniel Smith. If Mrs Smith's husband is dead or if she is divorced or separated then she is Mrs Mary Smith.

When you have sent an invitation to a guest to include a friend, it is important that you ask them their friend's name and that this is written in full, even if the best man has to carry a blank card in his pocket at the wedding and it is filled in at the last minute and put on the table. It is considered thoughtful and kind to do this sort of thing, rather than make people feel like strangers or an afterthought. The essence of good manners and being a good hostess is to make people feel welcome and at ease.

If you do not have very tidy handwriting, then it is better to ask a friend who does to write them or even type them yourself or ask someone to type them for you. Some people who have studied calligraphy will fill in place cards in beautiful script for you, but at a cost and it can be preclusively expensive.

QUANTITIES

One place card per guest is needed, but, again, do order extra. Sometimes guests who have said that they cannot come, suddenly decide that they can, or else after you have written some out a family may not be able to come due to illness and you may wish to invite someone else. Also when writing place cards it is extremely easy to make mistakes, so extras are needed for this.

BOOK MATCHES

Book matches which have the bride's and groom's names on can be obtained from the same suppliers as for the rest of the stationery, but these are obviously quite expensive. Over the past two years or so, there has been a marked decline in the requirement of these as some people feel that this is an encouragement to guests to smoke. The habit of putting cigarettes on the table for guests to help themselves has also virtually died out. Brides and Grooms sometimes feel that a book of matches will be useful over a day or two to their guests, thus prolonging the memory of their wedding, but generally speaking few people provide these today. If you do decide to order book matches, one per family should suffice.

THANK YOU LETTERS

Thank you letters must be sent promptly on return from honeymoon to *everyone* who gave you a present for your wedding. They need not be long in content, but should be handwritten. A basic letter which avoids thanking the wrong person for a certain present goes

Dear ....
Thank you very much (or .... [husband's name] and I would like to thank you very much) for your kind and thoughtful gift, which was much appreciated.
Yours sincerely,
(Bride's christian name, followed by her new name. It is wrong to put Mrs before your name or in brackets after.)

If you wish to you can mention the actual gift and instead of saying 'kind and thoughtful gift' you could say 'set of saucepans, which you so kindly gave us and which are in daily use'. Do not make the task more arduous than necessary by going into long dissertations about the wedding or your honeymoon.

If you use the more 'open' type of thank you letter, if you have sufficient time before your wedding, then you could actually start writing the thank you letters then. It may seem a bit mercenary, but if you want to do them all by hand it can be extremely strenuous trying to get all the thank you letters out promptly on your return from honeymoon.

PERSONALISED STATIONERY

It is possible to buy 'bridal notepaper' to handle any necessary correspondence during the period immediately prior to your wedding and for sending the thank you letters out on. With this it only has the Bride and Groom's christian names and the date of their wedding printed at the top, with a pattern to match the invitations. This is, of course, rather expensive and does not save you any handwriting, or typing.

I think it is preferable to purchase stationery which has the Bride and Groom's new address printed in the top right-hand corner as this saves you having to write the address out each time.

PRINTED CARDS

Printed cards are worded roughly the same as the 'thank you letter' I have suggested in the first part of this section. Although, it is preferable to send out handwritten letters, if there are a very large number of thank you letters to write, then it is better to get the printed cards as it is very quick and easy to send these out. You can write 'Dear . . . .' at the top of each one and sign it at the bottom, with a short personal note where you feel you want to, or write more on the back if you need to. But it is better to get these out quickly, making a note of those you want to send letters to and to write these at your leisure.

The printed cards can be obtained from most stationers, newsagents and card shops. The personalised ones, which also have the Bride's and Groom's name on are obviously more expensive than the 'off the peg' type, which can be bought in packets of six, ten and twelve.

If ordering the personalised printed ones, this should be done before the wedding, as with personalised writing paper, so that they can be sent out very soon after your return from honeymoon.

The most important thing to remember about thank you letters is that you must send them and you must post them off promptly.

It is not so necessary to over-order with thank you letters or cards as if you run out, you can send handwritten letters, so in order to work out numbers allow one card, or sheet of paper to every two guests, who came to your wedding.

STATIONERY

Invitations (number _____) £

Evening Invitations (number _____) £

Orders of Service (number _____) £

Serviettes (number _____) £

Place cards (number _____) £

Book matches (number _____) £

Cake boxes (number _____) £

Thank you cards (number _____) £

Total .... £

Deposit paid .... £

Balance due on _____ .... £

Appearance

Most people informed that there is to be a wedding immediately think 'What am I going to wear?' and this is a matter of extreme importance with the Bride. On a wedding day the Bride is the centre of attention, and she usually takes tremendous care in choosing the style of dress which she feels will suit her best. If she chooses to wear white, then nobody else wears that colour. The Bride is the focal point of any wedding. She will be in almost every photograph and therefore her appearance is of paramount importance, coming a close second is the Groom, closely followed by the Bridesmaids and Best Man.

However, dress is not the only thing to think about, there are hair, footwear, hands (these are shown very close up in some photographs, plus everyone will want to see the Bride's wedding ring), skin, figure, make-up, and so on.

DRESS

Bride
Traditionally brides have worn white for about one hundred and fifty years. It was a fashion set by Queen Victoria and today most

brides choose to 'wear white, although cream is still a popular choice. Cream always seems a popular choice where the Bride has children or is being married for a second time either through divorce or widowhood. However, if a Bride still prefers to wear white there is absolutely no reason why she should not. There was a time when widows would wear grey or 'tender shades of mauve', but this is now considered rather démodée.

At registry offices dress for the Bride really is optional and I have seen everything from jeans to a full white wedding dress with a cathedral length train. However, the most popular alternative is always a really pretty suit.

Long dresses worn to registry office weddings do not normally have trains, because you have to sit down during the ceremony and a train can offer a number of complications. Also as you do not 'sweep' down the aisle, there is no opportunity for guests to appreciate the beauty of a train and it is, therefore, superfluous.

Veils also are unnecessary in a registry office as there is no appropriate moment to pull back the veil as one does in church, so most Brides tend to prefer a hat, usually with a wide brim, giving an Edwardian effect.

Winter Brides should also think very carefully about the cold weather. It is reasonable to say that it will not be warm enough for a Bride to stand around for about half an hour in a flimsy dress (most wedding dress bodices are fairly fine) except in the late spring and summer, which can be accounted as May to September.

Most Brides who are married in the winter tend to choose their wedding dresses in the late summer and forget to allow for the cooler weather. The obvious choice for a winter wedding is velvet trimmed with fur or swans down, but a summer wedding dress could be made or bought and a cloak made out of two metre widths of white velvet, turned over at the top with a cord run through (this could be white, silver or gold) and could be lined or unlined and trimmed with lace or fur or swans down. It could also be richly decorated with embroidery, beads or sequins. This can be made at very short notice. I ran up something similar in black velvet for an evening function once in a day. Also it is possible to buy very fine woollen underwear (Damart) which would not show under a delicate dress, but would keep a mid-winter Bride quite cosy, especially a vest. However unromantic this may sound, it is better than feeling freezing cold during the photographs and looking rather blue.

Footwear should be carefully considered too – for a winter Bride sandals are not appropriate.

Groom

There used to be an old joke which said 'Why when the Bride wears white for virginity does the Groom wear black?' It still is correct today for the Groom to wear black or at least a very dark colour, morning dress being very popular. Morning suits are usually hired rather than bought and the various stockists show a range of black, black and grey, silver grey, brown and blue.

The Groom will often choose brown if the Bride is to wear cream and certainly this does add a very nice touch. With morning suits the top hat is worn and gloves, although the gloves are usually carried.

On entering the church the hat is removed and carried by its brim, together with the gloves in the left hand, so that the other hand is free to shake hands. When the Groom approaches the altar he leaves his hat and his gloves in the pew.

Some men feel that morning dress is too formal and not being accustomed to wearing it, just simply feel awkward in it and therefore opt for a lounge suit, which should be a very dark colour.

In this case a hat is not worn. The shirt should be white and the tie pale blue or grey with little or no pattern. (If a dinner jacket is being worn, then a black bow tie should be worn with it.) The Best Man usually wears the same as the Groom as should the Ushers and both the Bride's and the Groom's fathers.

Pastel coloured suits and tweeds, etc. although very fashionable are really out of place for a Groom to wear as they are too casual to complement most Bridal gowns. A Groom in a black suit does set off the Bride in white to perfection. Pastel colours do not have this effect.

Today there is a fashion for the Groom to wear white as well as the Bride and this can look very nice indeed, but the main problem would appear to be the use of the suit after the wedding, although these can also be hired.

If the Groom does not usually wear a suit it is generally cheaper to hire one for the wedding, rather than buying one which he might never use after the wedding.

Bridesmaids

Bridesmaids traditionally wear pastel shades or match the Bride as in the Prince and Princess of Wales wedding. However, with winter weddings you should beware of the 'cold' colours of blue and green, because with no leaves on the trees and if the pictures are taken against grey brickwork in particular, the whole thing can look very 'grey', especially if the sky is overcast. Again in winter the temperature must be considered and this is why with winter weddings we find the Bridesmaids tend to wear velvet or satin in red, royal blue, emerald green or gold, although satin is not a good idea if there is a slightly overweight Bridesmaid. Alternatively, they need capes or cloaks to go over their dresses. Because of this, winter weddings tend to be more expensive as far as dressing is concerned. It should be mentioned, though, that the dress hirers do hire out fur capes, etc.

Traditionally Bridesmaids wear long dresses, whether they are adult or small children and if the Bride's dress follows a historical style, e.g. Elizabethan, Victorian (early or late i.e. crinoline or bustle) or Edwardian, etc., then it looks better if the Bridesmaids echo that style. If you are in any doubt, then the local library will probably be able to help. For example if the Bride is wearing an early Victorian crinoline and her Chief Bridesmaid (an adult) is wearing, perhaps a smaller crinoline, then a small Bridesmaid with a short dress and long pantaloons and a poke bonnet can look really attractive, perhaps carrying a flower basket.

Today more and more Bridesmaids are wearing short day or

cocktail type dresses, but this does look out of place when a Bride is wearing a long dress.

Bride's Parents

The Bride's father will usually wear something similar to the Groom, Best Man and Ushers.

The Bride's mother, however, is another matter and usually as much time and trouble is taken over her outfit as that of the Bride. For the summer, the traditional outfit is a matching dress and coat or dress and jacket. The Bride's mother never looks fully dressed in just a dress, especially a short-sleeved one. The Bride's mother normally wears a hat as well. At a summer wedding this would be a lightweight 'straw' type of hat, but never felt as this is for winter. The hat can either match the dress or the handbag gloves and shoes. When selecting a hat the Bride's mother and any other person for that matter should ask for the advice of the assistant if they are not absolutely sure how the hat should be worn.

For a winter wedding the Bride's mother can either wear a warm wool suit with a felt hat to either match the suit or the handbag, gloves and shoes, or sometimes a fur coat is worn, in which case a fur hat can be worn.

Basically, to look smart the Bride's mother should think in terms of two colours only, one colour for the accessories and another colour for the suit, coat, dress, etc. If wearing a skirt and jacket type suit, then it always looks smarter if the blouse matches the accessories.

Any colour can be chosen for the Bride's mother to wear, although she usually liaises with the Groom's mother, to make sure that they do not wear the same colour, or clash in any way, nor should they clash with the Bridesmaids. However, if the Bride is wearing white, then it is wrong for anyone else to wear white at a wedding and this includes the two mothers, although white accessories, or a white background with a pattern is usually acceptable. It is also considered wrong and extremely bad luck if anyone wears black to a wedding (the ladies, that is), although, again black accessories are acceptable. However a black hat, unless relieved by brightly coloured decoration, can look out of place.

For winter weddings it does look better if the mothers can wear bright, warm colours and for summer weddings pastel colours tend to be very popular, although there is a saying that women should never wear pink between the ages of twenty-one and sixty, as it tends to make you look older.

Groom's Parents
The Groom's parents follow exactly the same rules as the Bride's parents. Although traditionally in the past the Groom's family took a back seat; today the Groom's parents are usually treated equally with the Bride's and should dress accordingly. The Groom's parents will be photographed as much as the Bride's and they will also sit at the top table. Normally if there is a clash over who is to wear what colour, then the Groom's mother gives way. It is really desirable that the two mothers go shopping for their outfits together and, if possible, with the Bride (or the Bride should liase between her mother and the Groom's mother about colour schemes if this cannot be arranged). This shopping trip should take place after the Bridesmaids' outfits have been chosen, or at least the colour finalised. This can be a marathon task, but where the Bride and Groom are on a budget and there is only to be one Bridesmaid, or none at all, the other guests can help to add colour to the wedding by carefully selecting their outfits, especially the two mothers.

Other Guests
The other guests wear what they like, but it is not considered good style for any lady to wear white or black (black is also unlucky). Ladies wearing trousers would be frowned upon as well. Dresses, suits, etc. should be 'day' type and not cocktail; it is in order to wear jewellery, but not in the hair. Flowers should not be worn in the hair, unless on a hat.

All the men at a wedding should wear suits. Some men prefer to wear blazers and this is just about acceptable, but not jeans and never shirt sleeves, except for the smallest children. A jacket should always be worn and this should not be a cardigan. A wedding is a place to dress formally and not casually. It is a mark of respect for the seriousness of the occasion. If the Groom, Best Man, Fathers and Ushers are wearing morning-dress, then the other guests should also hire morning-dress, although this is more the exception than the rule these days as hire costs are so expensive.

BUYING 'OFF THE PEG' OUTFITS AND HIRING

Bride

Most major stores have bridal departments and there are wedding dress shops which specialise in bridal wear. Most of these sell the accessories as well. However, do not let yourself be sold to. Make sure that you like the dress and that you feel comfortable in it.

Many brides like to hire their wedding dresses rather than to buy a new one, which can cost hundreds of pounds, only to be worn for one day. The shops which hire wedding dresses usually charge about one third to a half of the retail price, and the dresses which are hired out are usually the more expensive wedding dresses, so it will normally cost in excess of £100 to hire a wedding dress, certainly a sum for which a cheaper wedding dress can be bought and one could be made for much less.

If you are hiring or buying, it is normal for the wedding dress to be 'fitted'. That is to say that it will have to be shortened, lengthened or taken in or let out slightly, so that it fits exactly and the shop will charge for this service.

If you are getting married at short notice, make sure that the Assistant is aware of the date and that they will have time to get the dress back to you in good time allowing a few days to alter it again if there are any problems. Also find out how much this service is going to cost.

When you go to collect your wedding dress check the alterations and make sure that they have been carried out in a workman-like manner. I have seen some absolutely awful alterations. Also try your wedding dress on again, no matter how little work may have been done and make sure that it looks right. When trying it on, let your mother help you into your wedding dress as she will on your wedding day, so that if you are not sure the way a piece of it goes on, especially the veil and headdress, you can ask the assistant then. I have seen all too many brides in a flap on their wedding day, because they cannot arrange the wedding dress the way the assistant had as they had forgotten what she did.

Bridesmaids

Basically what is said under 'Brides' applies to the bridesmaids' dresses as well. However, for small children, make sure that when you order a dress, especially if this is a long time in advance of a wedding, that you have allowed room for growing. Twelve-year-old girls have a way of burgeoning in all directions in a very short time. Younger children can suddenly shoot up or put on weight. Really with small children, selecting their outfits should be left until the last possible moment, or at least the fitting should be.

Hiring Bridesmaids' dresses can work out to be the cheapest solution, especially as rarely, if ever, are they worn again and Bridesmaids do not attach the same sentimental value to their dresses as the Bride does to hers.

Groom, Best Man, Ushers and Fathers

Today it is easy for men to buy suits 'off the peg' and indeed eighty per cent of men do, so unless the men really want to spend hundreds of pounds on specially tailored outfits then departmental stores and mens' outfitters are usually able to produce suitable attire. Suits can also be bought or hired from the same shops as the wedding dresses and although it is wrong for the groom to accompany the Bride when she buys her dress, the Bride does usually accompany the groom when he is selecting his outfit.

Again, suits should always be tried on in the shops where they have been bought after the final alterations have been completed, and arrangements to collect these should be made a good time before the wedding. It is no good picking up a suit on the day before the wedding only to find that it does not fit correctly. Also if buying your suit, or even hiring it, from a shop some distance from home, it is no good getting it home, only to find you have picked up the wrong one, or it does not fit correctly.

Morning dress is usually hired, but remember when hiring that arrangements must be made to get the clothes back to the shop after the wedding and it is probable that the Bride and Groom will be on honeymoon.

Mothers

Rarely do Mothers of the Bride and Groom hire their wedding outfits, although some may like to hire accessories such as furs. Some of the better dress hire shops do offer elegant outfits suitable for the occasion and some bridal wear shops carry a section of clothes for mothers too. However, if you do choose to buy, do make sure whatever you choose feels comfortable as well as looking good. If possible select an outfit you will want to wear again on another occasion, something classic which will not date too quickly.

SELECTING DRESS PATTERN AND FABRIC

If you decide to buy material and a pattern for you or someone else to make up, before setting out it is a good idea to have a long cold look at your wardrobe. See if there is a style which is predominant in your wardrobe. I know in mine most of my dresses are fitted to the waist, with slightly flared skirts, for example. Or perhaps there is one particular dress which has earned you a lot of compliments or which you particularly like. If so, then it is possible to take a dress apart to copy the pattern, with a long skirt. The dress can then be put back together. However, if this is not possible, just take a long look at what your 'style' really is, whether you normally wear a fitted style or whether you prefer a blouson top. Perhaps you favour a gathered skirt, or maybe an 'A' line. It is important to establish this, especially if you are having a dress made for you, or if you are going to make the dress yourself, because once you have made it, then, basically, you are stuck with it and it is too late if you find that you do not like yourself in the dress. When choosing a pattern, the designs are usually shown in sketch form and are shown on very tall, slim models. Very few of us follow that sort of shape, so although a pattern may look absolutely gorgeous in the sketch, it could look dreadful on you, so it is important to establish an idea in your own mind of what looks best on you. Another good idea is to go to some of the bridal shops and try on some of their dresses. While you are there, you might also find out how much they cost before pricing making up your own. It is just possible that there will not be much difference in the cost, especially if you intend to use a dressmaker.

Dress Patterns for the Bride

COMPLICATED

Although some dress patterns may look very complicated, I have always found that these are the easiest to work with as they give very detailed instructions of every stage, and the finished dresses do live up to expectations.

Vogue are probably the best known of these and they actually have Parisian designers to design wedding dress patterns for them, which when given a few personal touches of your own can give a great deal of impact and individuality, which is what most Brides are looking for in their wedding dresses. Vogue also tend to use photographs on the fronts of their patterns, which is a great deal less misleading, although again, these models are usually a standard size 12, so still take care.

It is important with these patterns that you follow the instructions to the letter and do not try to take short cuts, as you will not get the same effect.

SIMPLE

The simplest pattern manufacturers, who are probably the best known, are Simplicity and Style. Both offer excellent designs, which can, again, have your own personal touches added to them. They are easy to cut out and have easy instructions to follow as well as normally requiring less fabric. These patterns are probably the best for the beginner.

Fabrics

EASY TO WORK WITH

Cotton and poly-cotton (that is polyester/cotton) are probably the easiest fabrics to work with as are the lock-knit, jersey types of nylon, although these require a special ball-point needle attachment for the sewing machine. An Edwardian style wedding dress, that is one with a fitted bodice, long sleeves and a straight, or slightly gathered long skirt, can look very nice in a poly cotton. Pure cotton is slightly risky as this will crease when sat on and can look very untidy by the time you arrive at the Church.

DIFFICULT TO WORK WITH

Velvet is a fabric, which, unless you are accustomed to working with it, is one which should really be left to a professional. Special equipment is required to give a professional finish to a garment, which could be preclusively expensive. When the dress is sewn, the maker then has to go along all the seams and pull the pile out from the stitching, in this way the seams are virtually invisible. If you do decide to make a velvet dress yourself do be careful that you get the 'nap' the right way. To do this you have to brush the fabric with your hand and the way that it feels the smoothest is the direction of the nap – all of the material must fall in this direction. (This is when the ends of the pile are pointing down towards the floor on a garment.)

Silk, tafetta, brocade, chiffon, georgette and crepe are not easy to work with as they have a tendency to slip and pucker when being sewn by machine. The best way round this problem is to lay the pattern on the fabric and tack the pattern to the fabric and then to sew the dress with the pattern still tacked to it, or, if you need to use the pattern again for the Bridesmaids' dresses, to cut out pieces from more tissue paper and tack this to the fabric. This helps to cut down the amount of slipping and stretching. All edges must be overcast before you commence sewing as they will fray, leaving you insufficient fabric to go into the seams. A ball-point needle is also needed for these fabrics to avoid the fabric 'catching' on the needle, causing snags.

Bridesmaids

CHILDREN

Young bridesmaids, that is to say, normally under ten-years-old, can really steal the show. Most children can take most styles, most colours and most fabrics, although satin always looks a bit 'old' on small children. The favourite colours are pink, peach or apricot, lilac, blue and lemon. Green is becoming popular as are lavender and silver grey. If you want to carry red flowers, bridesmaids in pink or peach will look very odd and lilac can look rather strange too. Blue, green and grey can look 'cold' for the winter weddings and lemon or very pale yellow will look insipid in the winter although a deeper buttercup yellow or a deep gold will add colour. With winter weddings the deeper colours of red, royal blue and dark green are also worn, especially in velvet.

There is also a fashion for Bridesmaids to wear white or cream, the same as the Bride. However, cream Bridesmaids' dresses will look 'dirty' if the Bride is wearing white. I have also seen 'cafe au lait', a pale coffee colour, worn by Bridesmaids. All of these can look very nice, but contrast must be added through the flowers which should be as colourful as possible with plenty of leaves and other greenery.

Little children can wear very small patterns, but a fabric with a large pattern on it will tend to 'swamp' them.

For really small Bridesmaids (under about six years of age) a dress with a very full skirt with lots of petticoats to stiffen it, cut to just above the ankle, looks very nice and gives an early 'Victorian' appearance. This is also very convenient for a small child to wear.

When cutting the hems of Bridesmaids' dresses, it is important with young children to make sure that they have enough room to walk. I have seen all too many Bridesmaids come to grief nervously entering the church and tripping over the hems of their dresses, because they have looked down, making the front of their dresses slightly longer. They then land in a heap either on the Bride's train or on her veil, pulling it from her head. This can lead to tears, which is most undesirable on a wedding day, and a little forethought can avoid such disasters.

Probably the best and most popular design of Bridesmaids' dress is the 'Empire Line', which is where the skirt is gathered onto a short bodice, which ends just under the bust. This type of dress can be made in a pretty white polyester/cotton fabric with a small floral pattern on it and the colours in the pattern can be picked out in the flowers which the Bride and Bridesmaids carry.

ADULTS

The worse possible design for an adult Bridesmaid's dress is the 'Empire Line'. I have never seen a Bridesmaid over ten years old wear it well. Inevitably it makes the Bridesmaid look pregnant, and it was originally designed for this purpose – the Empire Line came into fashion after the wars with France, when the men returned and many women became pregnant. At one stage the fashion even went as far as women wearing a sort of cushion attached to their girdles to make them look pregnant or 'in an interesting condition' as it was said in those days. A better alternative to the empire line is the princess line, which is where the bodice still ends under the bust, but the skirt is cut on the cross and fitted into the waist with an 'A' line skirt.

Generally speaking small patterned fabrics do not suit older Bridesmaids either; they look better dressed in a plain colour so the little ones can wear print whilst the older ones wear a plain colour to pick up the colours in the print. One wedding which I saw which was very nice was where the Bride was dressed in white, so was the little Bridesmaid, but the older Bridesmaids wore a yellow and orange patterned fabric, where the pattern was scattered on a white background and everyone carried orange and yellow flowers with plenty of foliage.

The greatest mistake is the forgetting of petticoats. Most Brides get married in the summer when the light is very bright, those who do not, get married in the winter when the angle of light is very low. Consequently Bridesmaids should try on their dresses and stand in front of a very bright light, preferably sunlight to ensure that their dresses do not become transparent in daylight. The same applies to the Bride. I remember one wedding where as the Bride came out of church and turned to look back to have her photograph taken with her new husband, the sun was directly behind her and when the photograph came out she looked as though she was standing naked with a cage around her (she was wearing a crinoline), and the number of Bridesmaids who have had to go back to find petticoats, because as soon as they get out in the light to have their photographs taken their dresses have appeared transparent. Artificial light is not as strong as natural sunlight, so it is important that dresses are tried on in sunlight and that plain long petticoats are bought, because if dresses are transparent, then they will show a pattern or where a short petticoat or slip ends.

Use of Period Styles to Create an Effect

Many of today's wedding dresses are based on designs from periods of history, and the most popular are Victorian, Edwardian and even some Elizabethan. If you have selected a wedding dress from one of these periods of history, then it really does add a touch of authenticity to the whole affair if you go along to the library, and do a little research to see what other styles were popular at that time to use for the Bridesmaids.

Most reference libraries are quite happy to help with such searches, especially if you mention that it is for your wedding. If the Bride is to wear a crinoline, say, then perhaps for the Bridesmaids a smaller crinoline as worn for daywear at that time would be a good idea and if you want to dress young Bridesmaids, to look at what children were wearing at that time. This sort of thing gives a 'thought out' appearance to a wedding. Many Brides choose their Bridesmaids outfits and their own outfits on the basis of what they have seen before, taking one part of the outfit from one wedding they have seen previously and something else from another, without thinking about whether they go well together or not.

Another way to give the wedding a co-ordinated look is to use the same pattern or style for all the dresses, with small variations. Say for example the Bride is to wear an off the shoulder dress with a full skirt and a crinoline petticoat, then the adult Bridesmaids could have the same pattern, but in a colour, this colour being picked up in ribbon on the Bride's dress and/or in the flowers. The small Bridesmaids could then have the same pattern for the skirt, but with a fitted bodice with a yoke to echo the 'off the shoulder' effect, perhaps with lace along the seam, to pick this out and a ruffle at the neck. This little dress could be white with coloured ribbon as the Bride or coloured the same as the adult Bridesmaids or in a pattern. This gives a very 'complete' look to a wedding.

Mother of the Bride (or Groom)
The Mothers to the Bride and Groom have a great chance at a wedding to look really stunning and most mothers take the opportunity to do so.

Use of Colour
There are only two colours which are not worn at a wedding: white because it vies with the Bride, although a blouse or accessories in white are acceptable: and black, although black accessories are acceptable. However, a black blouse and a black hat, although very smart can still look a bit funereal. A wedding is a celebration and colours are normally worn. Also where there is little colour in the wedding, either through there being no Bridesmaids, or

because it is a winter wedding, then the mothers really do have a chance to make a big 'splash'. Some people are superstitious about green, it being the 'fairy' colour of ancient legend, but personally I love green in all its shades. However for the superstitious there are plenty of other colours to choose from, e.g. peacock blue, turquoise, various yellows, red, orange and pink (from palest dusty pink to crushed strawberry and cyclamen), royal blue (navy blue is a bit dark), silver grey (with red accessories this can look really interesting, especially on blondes) (the dark greys are a bit funereal and not very exciting), lilac and lavender (deep mauves can look funereal too, but it all depends on how they are accessorised).

Use of Style

Many Brides' mothers just do not seem to put the time and thought into their outfits that the occasion demands. Again, as with the Bride, if choosing a pattern or having an outfit made, then the Bride's mother or Groom's mother should take a long look at her wardrobe to decide what style does suit her best, rather than just choosing something that looks good in the pattern book. Trying on a few outfits in their favourite stores is a good idea too. When choosing fabrics only the slimmest should choose clinging fabrics and these should be checked for 'static cling'.

Large ladies usually look better in tailored styles rather than the 'blouson' styles, which tend to make them look 'all bunched up' in the middle.

Make sure when having an outfit made or when buying one off the peg that there is plenty of room in it. It is important to remember that a large meal is going to be eaten and tummies do expand at such times. Do not select anything where there could be trouble with straps slipping or with a scarf which might keep moving around. If you do, then it is a good idea to have these stitched on, even if it is with a couple of invisible tacking stitches after you have put it on. It is better than having to fiddle with a part of your outfit during the wedding. Also avoid anything strapless as this sort of garment usually requires special underwear, which can be uncomfortable to wear. If any new underwear especially brassieres and girdles are purchased for the occasion, they should be checked under the outfit they are bought to support and worn for a while around the house to ensure comfort. If a Bride's mother faints it is usually less likely to be through emotion than through an over-tight girdle. Also do remember that summer wedding days can be quite hot and check that you are not wearing more undergarments than is necessary; cotton or silk will keep you the coolest.

Fitting and Cutting

THE PATTERN

When you buy your dress pattern the likelihood is that you will buy a standard size 12, 14, 16 – whatever size you buy your dresses. However, very few of us are a standard size, so the thing to do is to pin the pattern onto you so that you can be sure of fitting it to you. I know that although I buy a standard dress size off the peg, when making a dress I take two inches off the back and put two inches into the front. It is still the same measurement round the bust. Also if you have bought the wrong size, then it is cheaper to buy a new pattern at this stage than to have to buy new fabric because the dress has been cut too small. Mark the pattern if it needs taking in or letting out, making alterations to the darts if the bust size is wrong and to the skirt if any alterations need making to the waist, ensuring that you are keeping all seams in line.

TACKING

It is absolutely imperative that all parts of the pattern are tacked to the fabric. Pin the pattern on first and then tack it on. This will avoid the pattern slipping, when cutting out the dress. Then carefully mark all the other darts and marks on the pattern, where pieces are meant to meet each other. This is done with 'tailors' tacks'. This is when the needle is passed through the fabric and the pattern over the fingers (two fingers) and back through the fabric and pattern. This is done three times, leaving a long end. When you then wish to separate two pieces of the dress you slide the top piece upwards and cut through the middle of the tacks in between the two pieces of fabric. This way you will have ensured that each piece is marked evenly on the other side. When making tailors tacks remember to allow for any alterations which may have been necessary when you tried the pattern on. Also allow a little extra on all the seams as these can be trimmed off later and re-overcast.

Now you should overcast all the raw edges to prevent fraying.

All these steps may seem time consuming, but they do save time and trouble later on.

CUTTING

When cutting your dress you need plenty of time and no interruptions as a mistake at this time can be expensive. Open the scissors up and make long cuts – this avoids a 'jagged' edge. Cut carefully and concentrate.

FITTING

Next you should separate all the pieces of the dress, tacking them to tissue if necessary to avoid the fabric stretching or slipping, and then tack the whole dress together, leaving out zips and fastenings and try the dress on. If it is too big you need someone to pin it on you. The dress is tried on 'inside-out'. Then retack the alterations. Do the bodice first and finish retacking that before you try on the skirt with it, then get the skirt to fit the bodice. Do not remove any extra material from seams. Now you are ready to sew the seams. When you have done this, again keeping the bodice and the skirt separate, try the bodice on and then the skirt, if nothing needs altering, then you can join the skirt and the bodice.

Each time you try the garment on, pin the openings where fasteners, i.e. zips, etc. will go. Once you have put the whole dress together, try it on again, provided everything looks right, then you can put the zip in, but do this carefully as a badly finished zip opening can ruin a dress. Again, pin the zip in first, then tack it in, and then sew it in.

Now you can trim off any extra material, leaving sufficient fabric in the seams, just in case you put on a little extra weight. never make a dress too small in anticipation of losing weight through dieting. Try the diet first and then make your dress. Nothing looks worse than a dress which is under pressure from its contents (i.e. you)!

Now you can make any petticoats, crinolines (or borrow one), sashes, etc. and then try the whole thing on together, and get someone to mark the hem for you. Make sure that you are standing straight as the hem is marked and if you feel yourself beginning to 'droop', stop for a while, take the dress off if necessary, and sit down. With some dresses, marking the hem can be a very long and tiring business, so it is better to do it right the first time, rather than take it off and look at it and realise that it is all wrong. Now tack the hem up roughly and check it again by trying it on. If you are wearing a crinoline, it is important that this is tried on under the dress every time the hem is checked as it varies the shape of the hem.

When the hem looks even, you can trim it and tack it up properly, and then hem it, preferably by hand, unless there is lace or an overlay to go over the top. Then you must press your dress, making sure the seams are not puckered in any way.

Use of dressmaker's dummy

Some dressmaker's dummies are not very expensive and can be altered to match your own form. Most of them have instructions with them to tell you how to use them.

Some fabric shops hire these out, or you may be able to borrow one. These are very useful as they give you an idea of how the dress is taking shape and enable you to check things as you go along, especially if you have nobody who can easily help you.

Bridesmaids' dresses

The same rules for making the Bridesmaids' dresses should be followed as those under 'Fitting and Cutting' for the wedding dress, however, there are a couple of things to bear in mind.

WHEN TO MAKE THEM OR BUY THEM

With adult bridesmaids it is not such a problem to buy or make their dresses in advance, as it is unlikely that they will put on weight or grow in any way, although if you are making dresses for children, remember that they are apt to grow at a phenomenal rate and their dresses should never be made or ordered more than three months in advance, and even then deep seams and hems should be allowed, in case anything needs letting out or down. Girls between ten and fourteen can quite suddenly develop busts, so the selection of their dresses should be left as late as possible.

DRESSES FOR BRIDESMAIDS WHO LIVE A LONG WAY AWAY

If you are buying dresses for Bridesmaids who live a long way away then the best thing to do, if the Bridesmaids cannot come to you and you cannot go to them, is to buy them from one of the chains like Pronuptia or Berkertex, by selecting them from the brochure and letting the Bridesmaid go to get her own dress and have it altered at her nearest branch.

If the dresses are to be made, then it is better if the pattern and fabric are sent to her so that she or her mother or some other relative can make it or, if this is not possible, she can get a dress-maker to make it for her. This may sound expensive, but if the distance is very great, then the cost of travel for three fittings can be greater.

Decoration of Dresses

There are many ways to decorate a dress whether it is for the Bride or her Bridesmaid, and decoration can be added not only to a hand-made dress, but also to shop bought dresses and even dresses which have been bought second-hand. This can add a very individual touch, especially to a chain store dress and is a way of introducing a little colour to the wedding dress, if this is desired, to give a co-ordinated appearance.

RIBBON

As ribbon is used in the floristry as well, it can be a reasonably inexpensive way of introducing colour, decoration and individuality to a wedding dress. Say, at a wedding where the Bridesmaids are in a pale pink and the Bride in white and she wishes to have pink and lilac flowers, then the Bridesmaids could have lilac and white ribbon banding, say, their skirts and around their puff sleeves. The Bride wearing a plain crepe dress with a hooped skirt and elbow length puff sleeves could have three bands of pink and two bands of lilac narrow ($\frac{1}{4}-\frac{1}{2}$ in) ribbon alternating around her skirt and around her sleeves, with three bands around, say, a square neck. The Bridesmaids would only have three bands each. The flowers would have the ribbons amongst them and trailing down behind the bouquets.

LACE

Lace is probably the most popular method of decorating a dress for a wedding. Sometimes the lace is used as an overlay, covering the entire dress. It can be applied sparingly to only the edges, or the motif can be cut out and appliqued onto either the bodice or the skirt, or more thickly on the bodice and more sparsely on the skirt, or only to one part of the dress, such as the sleeves and the train. The train may be covered in ruffles of lace, with motifs appliqued to the skirt and bodice and a length of lace ruffled onto the hem of the skirt. There are many alternatives which when carefully executed can give an original and stunning effect.

FLOWERS

Flowers are usually used to 'hitch' a skirt up to display the petticoats beneath. The petticoats could be coloured or white for the Bride with the main dress white and the flowers the same as the bouquets. The Bridesmaids could have coloured dresses with white petticoats. Flowers can also be applied to shoulders, the décolleté of a dress, to a sash at the side, in front with the ends of the sash hanging in the front, or as a posy in the middle of the back either instead of a bow or as well as. Flowers, small ones, can be scattered over a train or stitched onto a dress in a 'garland' across the front, forming a graceful curve. Again there are very many ways to use flowers in an original manner, which would automatically give a co-ordinated look as the same flowers would be used in the bouquets.

EMBROIDERY

The quantity of embroidery used on dresses these days is negligible, so the Bride deciding to use this method of decorating her dress can be sure that the dress will be quite unique. But the quantity of embroidery to be used would depend on the skill of the embroiderer and the time available for its completion.

The embroidery could be in white, or again, could pick up the Bridesmaids' colour. One extremely unique wedding dress I saw was where a relative of the Bride, who was a skilled embroiderer, had copied the motif from the fabric worn by the Bridesmaids in embroidery onto the wedding dress and veil and this really did look very good.

The Bridesmaids had their dresses made to the same pattern and design as the Bride's. It is also quite inexpensive, but very effective to appliqué pieces of satin onto a dress either in the shape of flowers or leaves or butterflies; the possibilities are endless.

BEADS, PEARLS AND SEQUINS

Beads and sequins are becoming popular again, especially glass beads, because they reflect the light, which can give a startling effect on a summer's day. These can be applied in a scattered fashion on one part or all of a gown, or can be formed into patterns. Diamantés, glass beads and sequins can also be sewn onto silk flowers in a bouquet also to reflect the light and will appear like early morning dew. Pearls are becoming very popular again, both as jewellery and as decoration. These can be used to draw attention to a lace motif, like the centre of a flower, or as an edging or scattered or used to form a design.

COMBINATIONS

The combinations of the above decorations are endless and there are no hard and fast rules, except not to allow your design to become too cluttered and fussy. Lace and pearls together, flowers and ribbon appliquéd to a dress with a diamante on each flower is a possibility, embroidery with pearls and glass beads. This is the time to think out your own decoration and remember your budget. Embroidery is probably the cheapest if you have a selection of silks, but if not it can be expensive, but do check that you can still get the same colours if you have had your silks for some time.

Headwear

VEILS

The veil is still very popular and is still recognised as being symbolic of the Bride and her chastity. Although veils have been used for hundreds of years there are times when they have not been worn at all. Roman Brides used to go veiled to their weddings.

The length of the veil should be considered very carefully. The most popular lengths are: shoulder length, fingertip length, floor length (either to the hem of the dress or just slightly longer) and cathedral length, which extends beyond the length of the train. Most of these are a matter of taste, but the cathedral length veil is usually only worn when there is a train to a dress and is really not appropriate when there is any likelihood of bad weather, as in the winter, when it can become very muddy and wet, which can ruin the whole effect of the wedding. The same goes for a long train.

Veils are normally made of tulle, edged with lace and can be highlighted with sequins or beads. Ideally the fabric should not be so dense that it obscures the features of the Bride.

Some Brides prefer to go to the church with the veil over their face, lifting it when the Register is signed, and to walk back down the aisle with their new husband. However, the veil can be pulled back when the Chief Bridesmaid takes the flowers from the Bride. The Chief Bridesmaid can do it herself by firstly handing her own bouquet to another Bridesmaid before going forward to help the Bride. She should pull the veil back before she takes the Bride's bouquet. It is perhaps preferable to do this when the weather is very hot. The Bride need not, under these circumstances, have pulled the veil forward until just before she enters the church, although this is normally done before she leaves the house.

HEADDRESSES

Headdresses can be worn with or without a veil. They can be made of pearls, diamantés (the lucky have family tiaras set with diamonds) or small silk flowers. Really, it is not possible to make these to compare with the bought varieties. However, some pretty headdresses can be made from silk or fresh flowers. Fresh flowers do tend to be a bit heavy, but provided care is taken to use small flowers and to keep the headdresses delicate, then silk flowers can be used. These can then match both the Bride and the Bridesmaids' flowers and can work out quite economical, but it should be pointed out that they can be quite time consuming to make as they are very fiddly.

When buying Bridesmaids and Brides headdresses, it is important that care is taken to find out how they fit onto the head. Rarely are combs sufficient and they therefore need extra support from hair grips. With children, when they have fine hair, it can be very difficult to find enough hair for the headdress to fit to and with skull caps in particular children can find them uncomfortable, if not painful to wear. If you are buying your headdresses, then find out from the shop how they are meant to be attached to the head. If there is no obvious answer, then a piece of tape run round the inside of the cap, or a crocheted chain inside a fine headdress of flowers, sewn carefully and invisibly, leaving gaps for the hairgrips to go through will help.

Headdresses are best attached to the hair by the hairdresser on the morning of the wedding.

Ensure that your veil is carefully and neatly attached to the headdress and try it on first. If you are having a full circlet head-dress then the veil should be attached at the back of the circlet, about one-third of the way across a full circle veil, so that the veil can be pulled forward. The veil should never be put on the head with the headdress over the top, because when it is pulled back it gives a very strange looking effect.

Please make sure that your veil is securely attached to the head-dress. There is nothing worse than having the two come apart just as you are leaving the house.

HATS

Hats are very popular today, especially when it is not the first time a girl is to be married. However, hats do have their down-falls. The most popular type of hat is the wide brimmed 'Ascot' type of hat, decorated either by the manufacturer or by the Bride with either feathers or flowers to match her bouquet. Ribbon can also be used. A hat band of ribbon either the same or slightly narrower, but the same colour as that used for the Bride's sash, with a few flowers the same as her bouquet, can be very effective. A hat base covered in the same fabric as the Bride's dress could be used.

The main problem with hats is that they tend to cause shadows over the Bride's face, especially the broad brimmed variety. A very dense fabric can virtually obscure the Bride's face. Loosely woven or lacy fabrics can give a mottled shadow, which tends to make the Bride appear to have some unspeakable kind of skin disease. So hats should always be tried on under a bright overhead light, preferably bright sunlight.

Using a Dressmaker

SELECTING A DRESSMAKER

The best way to find a dressmaker is through recommendation, but if you have not seen any of her work you should ask to see photographs or arrange to go to see dresses she may be making between making the arrangements and actually having the work done, to ensure that her workmanship is the standard you would wish. If you are not very experienced in these matters, then take someone with you who is.

Do not be afraid to ask for an estimate of how much it is going to cost. You will need this for price comparison anyway. Find out whether she can get your fabric cheaper for you or the sundries, like zips, buttons, decorations. Try to get at least two quotations from dressmakers for making the dresses.

Most dressmakers will ask for at least three fittings, but find out if there will be any extra charge if more fittings are needed.

GETTING A DRESSMAKER TO HELP

If you start to make your own dress or the Bridesmaids' dresses and you find that things are not working out as they should, or you are running out of time, then do not be afraid to admit failure and contact a dressmaker to help you. They will, of course, charge for their work, but it is better than carrying on and maybe losing sleep over it. Your time can always be spent more economically elsewhere.

Dressmaking is not difficult, but a wedding dress is rather special and a bigger job than most of us will ever have to do again.

Hairdressers

BEFORE

Once you have selected your headdress and veil, it is time to consult your hairdresser. Take your headdress and veil along to the hairdresser and let him see it. If you are going to wear your hair up or change your hairstyle in any way at all, get him to try the style for you to make sure that you like it that way. Never, ever have a new hairstyle on your wedding day, because if you do not like it, it is too late to change. The same goes for having your hair cut. You should allow him to cut the style months before your wedding, so that if it does not suit you you have time to let it grow out. It should be recut about a fortnight before your wedding to give your hair time to 'settle down' again.

Generally speaking, I always feel that the Bride's hair should surround her face and that although pinned up styles look fine for evening wear, something less sophisticated looks better for a wedding. Very short hair can also be a problem as it is difficult to grip a headdress to it and, again, it can look rather severe.

Never change the colour of your hair for your wedding, or suddenly decide to have streaks put into it, or highlights. Once again, it could be that you will not like the effect and you will not have time to change it. Also people will expect to see you as you really are and as they know you and it looks better if you comply with this. Remember also that some people are allergic to perms and dyes, and particularly when you are excited or nervous you could develop an allergy to one of these.

The condition of your hair is important as you want it to look healthy and shiny, so you should make regular appointments to see the hairdresser and get him to condition it. When you wash it yourself also use a conditioner. Regular visits to the hairdresser will enable him to become accustomed to you and your hair and the result will be much better than relying on him just to blow-wave your hair on the morning of your wedding.

THE MORNING OF YOUR WEDDING DAY

Try to book your hairdresser's first appointment, especially if you have to cope with your own catering, or if you have any other work to do before you get married. Many Brides think that to make an appointment about three hours before the wedding is sufficient, but it really is not. An hour for the hairdresser, an hour to get ready and an hour for the photographer. If you are held up at the hairdressers, then this can mean a rush to get ready, or being late for the photographer. It is best to get up and have your bath and go straight to the hairdresser. If your mother is also to visit the hairdresser and the Bridesmaids, then get them there with you. That way you will know that when this session is over all everyone has to do is to apply their make-up and dress.

You should take your headdress and veil with you (the veil being firmly fixed to the headdress) and let the hairdresser put it on for you. In that way you can be sure that it will be securely fixed and the hairdresser will be able to cover the pins. This is a bit of a problem if you have a long veil and are doing your own catering, so do think very carefully when selecting your headdress and veil about your commitments for the rest of the day. The Bridesmaids should also have their headdresses fitted at the hairdresser's.

Beauticians

FIGURE

Your figure is something which needs to be looked at long before selecting a wedding dress. If you feel you are overweight you should select a sensible, careful diet, over a long period of time. Crash diets are not a good idea as they tend to make you feel tired at a time when you need all your energy and they tend to be vitamin deficient, which can affect the condition of your hair and skin, which are equally, if not more important than your figure.

It is possible that all you will need is to tone up some muscles which have fallen into disuse and many beauticians have passive exercise machines, which will do this for you. If this is too expensive just start walking more, say, to the station and to the shops on a Saturday and taking a walk during your lunch hour. The fresh air will do you good as well. You could start to go swimming once a week, or go for a very short 'jog' (especially if you do not run normally).

You could join an exercise class or take up yoga, but no violent exercise, especially if you are not used to it, like squash or weight training because you could injure yourself and not be able to complete the work you have to do for your wedding, or you could make yourself so tired that you cannot get on with your work.

It is far better to take light exercise, like walking, which should make you feel more energetic.

SKIN

The skin can be treated in two ways – internally and externally.

Internally through what you eat and what you do, externally through treatment and cosmetics.

You will probably find that by starting an easy diet and walking more, your skin will improve anyway. Salads and fruit will always help to clear a bad skin. Fresh air and swimming tend to help as well. But if you do have a real problem skin, then you can consult your doctor who may advise antibiotics or some other form of treatment. Vitamin tablets can sometimes help. The multi-vitamin kind are good, but not those containing iron. You should never take iron unless it is prescribed for you. Or another alternative is Brewers Yeast tablets. These can be bought from most chemists or health food shops and are just tablets made out of yeast.

If you smoke and drink alcohol, then a reduction in these will improve the condition of your skin and hair. Cutting them out altogether will be even better. Treating the skin externally is another matter. If you are getting married in late summer, then you should have the opportunity to lay out in the sun and to get a light suntan, but do not overdo it, because you could cause your skin to peel, giving a very unsightly appearance, or encourage freckles. Excessive exposure to the sun can make the skin leathery as well, which is not desirable.

Many beauticians have sunbeds where you can acquire a tan, but any course of treatment should be commenced well before your wedding, and topped up just before, but beware of skin reactions, especially if you use sun tan oils or creams. If you normally use one which you know suits your skin, do not suddenly change to another just prior to your wedding.

Many beauticians have specialist treatments for dry skin, oily skin and acne, most of which have some effect on the problem. There are many good cosmetics available for the treatment of these problems as well, but a good twice-daily skin routine should be commenced immediately the decision to marry is taken. That is to say, the cleanse, tone moisturise system. In the morning you should use a good cleanser or you can wash with a gentle soap, then use a toner and a good moisturiser. It is medically accepted that moisturisers do have a beneficial effect on the skin. At night you should cleanse (with a greasy or spotty skin wash with a mild unperfumed soap after cleansing), then use your toner and then a night cream, but if you cannot afford a night cream, use your moisturiser again.

Twice weekly you can use a face pack if you need it. If you feel the need, an eye cream can be used twice a week as well. never use moisturiser around the eyes as it tends to make them 'puffy'.

Never have a face pack less than three days before your wedding, in case this draws out the impurities and forms spots. Three days gives you the opportunity to get rid of them.

MAKE-UP

There are very few Brides who would consider themselves 'dressed' without make-up and most girls feel that they would like something special for the big day and consequently tend to wear a heavy, 'evening' type of make-up, which is obviously wrong as they will be married during the day.

EYES

The best colour eye shadow to go with white is green. Many people shudder at the thought of green eye shadow as it can look very out-of-date. But it should be carefully and delicately applied over the lid with a slightly darker green in the crease of the eyelid and to the outside corners. I find that the more expensive make-up manufacturers make more subtle colours and it could be a good idea to invest in a couple of new eyeshadows well before your wedding day, so that you have time to experiment. However, do ask the assistant's advice. Some companies will even do a full make-up for you free of charge and perhaps you can go back each week to buy one item, so that you have the full set for your wedding day, but do give yourself time to practice and, if necessary, ask the assistant to show you again how she did it.

Never use cream or pearl eye shadows, especially as highlighters on the brow-line. If a photographer uses a flash-gun this can light up like head-lights, or they can make your eyes look swollen and puffy.

LIPS

Never use a lipstick with a blue or mauve tint to it. This is not flattering in photographs, and tends to make a fair-skinned person look ill. Also a very dark lipstick and nail varnish can be a bit too 'obvious', so that the rest of your face pales into insignificance. Use red, coral, or pink lipsticks. Always use a lipbrush to apply your lipstick, drawing the outline first and then blot firmly by pressing a tissue in between your lips and closing your lips firmly on it. Then if the colour is not dark enough apply another layer. If you wish, you may apply lipgloss. In this way you can be sure that no matter how much you are inclined to lick your lips, the colour will remain. If you are not used to wearing lipstick or this method of applying it, do try it out a few times beforehand to get it right.

FACE MAKE-UP

Your face make-up should not be more than one or, perhaps, two shades darker than your own skin. If you have a sallow skin, then try one of the peachy shades. Ask the assistant for her advice, but note that artificial light can make a colour look much paler. Especially it you buy expensive cosmetics, it is a good idea to try testers on your skin and look at the results in the daylight before making a choice.

SPOTS

There are a number of preparations on the market to cover up spots and it is a worthwhile investment to have one of these standing by, just in case, especially if you know you are inclined to get spots. However, if one or two do appear, do not apply make-up too thickly, as this tends to make it go 'shiny' and so only draws attention to it.

BLUSHER

A powder blusher is probably the best as cream ones tend to look shiny and, again, get the assistant to show you the best way to apply it for your face. Do not assume that just because you have always worn your blusher a certain way that that is the best way to wear it. Blusher should be applied sparingly and not so that you look 'flushed', nor in a straight dark line in the cheek recesses, which can make you look ill, and gaunt. If you are trying a new blusher, again, you must practice with it until you get it right.

FACE POWDER

Very few people wear powder these days, but if you decide to wear powder, then the light 'transluscent' types are the best. Powder is particularly useful if you have a greasy skin and you know that you are inclined to 'shine' after a short while.

The powder should be applied after the eyeshadow, taking the face powder over the eyelids, which helps to 'set' the eye make-up, but before the powder blusher.

If you are using cream blusher, this is applied before the face powder, but slightly darker than normal, as the powder will 'tone-down' the cream blusher. The powder should be 'dotted' over the face with a cotton wool ball and then with a fresh one evenly distributed over the face, brushing any excess off.

MASCARA

Very few girls do not wear mascara and the colour is a matter of choice, although the bright colours of blue, green and mauve do appear to be out of place at a wedding. The best colours are black, brown and brown/black or grey. You should apply mascara by building it up in layers, making sure each time you apply it that all the eyelashes are separated.

HAND–CARE

Hands are very important at a wedding. In close-up photographs the hands will come into view and everyone will want to see your wedding ring as well, so it is important to have nice looking hands, so if you bite your nails, now is the time to stop.

The best way I know to stop biting your nails is to restrict yourself on each subsequent week by one finger, but letting yourself bite the rest. Commencing with the thumbnails, do not bite these for one week. Add the first fingers to these for the second week and carry on this way until you reach the fifth week when all you have left to chew are two little fingernails and all of your other nails should have started growing by now.

I have used this system a great number of times and it really works. Grooms who chew their nails can try the same method.

If you have dry skin on your hands, then you can go to work with the hand cream and really start looking after your hands now, wearing gloves in cold weather and when gardening or doing housework.

It is not necessary to varnish your fingernails for your wedding, but if you want to you should keep the colour light or bright, never dark. However, whether varnishing or not, give yourself a good manicure the day before your wedding, allowing about an hour in which to do it. If you are varnishing your nails, then make sure you allow yourself enough time with nothing to do in order to let them dry; smudged nail varnish can look awful.

TEETH

When getting married a visit to the dentist is important, especially to the hygienist. If you have not been to the dentist for some time, make an appointment for about a month before your wedding, so that any treatment can be done and forgotten before you get married. This is important as nothing is worse than toothache on your wedding day. This advice is not for Brides alone. Also you should see the hygienist as most wedding dresses are a very bright white and can make teeth look very yellow, so do check this out when buying your dress. Some people have teeth which are very yellow anyway, if you are one of these, it might be a good idea to have a cream wedding dress, or at least off-white, instead.

Appearance

Shoes and Feet

On your wedding day you will be on your feet nearly all day, whether you are doing everything yourself or not. If you have any problems with your feet, then you should see your doctor or chiropodist.

Make sure your shoes are comfortable when you buy them and that the heels are not too high for you. Never buy a heel higher than you are used to wearing (a quick check of your 'day-to-day' shoes will tell you your normal heel height) as you will not walk well in them and they will make your feet ache. Having purchased a pair of shoes, they must be 'roughed-up' first, and then do wear them around the house to 'break them in'. In this way you will soon find out if they are not comfortable and you can be sure they will not pinch on the day, no matter how hot you get. Bear in mind that you will be wearing a very heavy, long dress, which puts more weight onto your feet, as well as enclosing them, which can make your feet swell.

If you know your feet are inclined to swell, then strappy shoes, especially those with ankle straps are not a good idea, as they will tend to 'cut'. It really is important to make sure that your feet are comfortable on your wedding day as you cannot enjoy yourself if your feet are uncomfortable.

If you are getting married in the winter, then think about footwear very carefully. Sandals are obviously wrong as your feet will be cold and probably wet. Remember although it may not be a wet day, it is rare in the winter for the ground to be dry, unless it is solidly frozen. Bridesmaids footwear should be thought about in this light too. If you are to be married in January, February and even March, it is possible for snow to be on the ground. There are some very pretty ankle boots and even knee length boots which could be worn under such circumstances. Remember the Victorians and Edwardians usually wore boots under their long dresses!

APPEARANCE

Bride

Wedding Dress £

Shoes £

Veil £

Headdress £

Underwear £

Petticoat £

Parasol £

Gloves £

Miscellaneous (new cosmetics and perfume, etc.) £

Bridesmaids

Dresses £

(Metres of fabric main _____ @ £_____ per metre £

Metres of Lining _____ @ £_____ per metre £

Zips _____ @ _____ each £

Buttons _____ @ _____ each £

Lace _____ metres @ _____ per metre £

Ribbon _____ metres @ £_____ per metre £

Dressmaker's services £_____ per dress £

Total £_____

Shoes £

Headdress £

Slips £

Gloves £

Parasols, bags, bibles, etc. £

Presents No. ___ of _____ @ £_____ each £

No. _____ of _____ @ £_____ each £

Groom

Suit £

Shirt £

Tie £

Shoes £

Underwear/socks £

Present for Best Man £

Total £_____

The Cake

BUYING A CAKE

The most important thing to remember when ordering a cake is to ask to have it delivered a week early. There are two very good reasons for this.

The first is that it saves you time in that last very busy week. The second reason is much more important and that is that the biggest disaster which commonly occurs at a wedding is that of the 'toppling wedding cake'. This usually happens because the icing on the cake is still wet. Not necessarily on top, but underneath, so that the soft inner layer of the icing on the bottom tier gives way when the weight of the other two tiers is placed on top of it for any length of time. If you collect your cake a week in advance, then even if the confectioner who made it left the icing until the last minute, then it still has a full week to dry out. This is such an easy and inexpensive way to make sure that nothing can go wrong, I cannot understand why everyone does not take this precaution. —

Staining appearing on the icing

If during the week any stains start to appear on the icing, this is because the marzipan was not properly dried out or sealed before the cake was iced and you should immediately take the cake back to the person who iced it. They will then have to strip off the decoration and re-ice the cake, replacing the decoration. This will not be your fault and it is the confectioner's responsibility.

Keeping the cake

When you receive your cake it should be boxed, but if not (amateurs do not always use boxes) then find some cardboard boxes (you can sometimes pick up some from the supermarkets but not boxes from soaps, soap powders, etc. as these can 'taint' the cake) and place the cake in these and then keep them in a cool dry place away from the sunlight.

MAKING THE CAKE YOURSELF

Many quite good cooks fight shy of making a wedding cake, when, as they are so very expensive to buy these days, a real economy can be made by making one yourself. The reason wedding cakes are so expensive is not because of the ingredients, although these are dear enough, but because of the amount of time it takes to ice a cake, so if you have plenty of time there is no reason why you should not have a go. The method of icing we suggest you use is the 'rolled out' type. When dry it is virtually indistinguishable from royal icing, but as the main reason people do not make their own wedding cakes is because they are nervous about flat icing with royal icing, then this method of icing really does give the person with little or no experience a chance of producing a very 'professional' looking job.

It is a good idea, if you have not tried this type of icing before, to practice on a Christmas or Birthday cake, using the design you intend to pipe on your wedding cake. This will give you a good idea of the problems involved before you start. In actual fact, you will probably find that making a smaller cake first and trying this method of icing will put your mind at rest!

The Cake

Preparations

Before you start, make sure that you have all the equipment and materials you will need. Also make sure that you have enough time to finish the job. It takes about six hours to bake the bottom tier of a wedding cake.

First think about what shape you are going to have – round or square. Horseshoes and hearts are very difficult to flat ice, so unless you are very experienced at cake decorating, it is better to forget about these shapes.

Next think about how many tiers. A 10 in bottom tier will cut to about 100 portions of wedding cake, and a three tier using a 10 in base cuts to about 200 portions. The custom of keeping the top or middle tier for the christening of the first child is dying out now, so many Brides feel that a two tier cake is sufficient. For a small wedding where no more than 120 portions will be required a bottom and a top tier, makes the most attractive proportion, and I always think the bottom and top tier together look best. However, where about 150 portions or more of wedding cake are required then you can use the bottom and middle tier size cake tins.

The ideal sizes for a three tier cake are 12 in, 9 in and 6 in (round or square). Square cakes take a larger volume of mix than round tins of the same dimension, but these make a rather large cake and I would suggest a better combination would be 10 in, 8 in and 6 in or in a square 9 in, 7 in and 5 in (this would give the same quantity of cake as the 10 in, 8 in and 6 in in the round and both would be sufficient for 200 portions).

It is obviously best to arrange the cake to fit in with any cake tins you already have as buying three cake tins can work out very expensive. If you do not have suitable tins, these can be hired.

If you only have one 'middle size' cake tin it is possible to make a 'three tier' cake with this by making three cakes the same size and using two at the bottom and having the 'top tier' stradling the two bottom ones on cake pillars, with two cake pillars on each of the bottom two cakes. This can give an unusual and unique touch to a wedding. Again, this would cut to about 200 portions.

For small weddings, some Brides decide to have a one tier wedding cake, but I always feel that for the very little extra expense involved, a two tier cake looks much more exciting.

EQUIPMENT
Tins
Pastry brush
Large amount of Greaseproof paper
Oil (vegetable) or vegetable fat
Scissors
Pencil
Foil
Mixing Bowl
Wooden spoon or electric mixer
Metal Spoon
Scales
Small plastic or glass bowls (two)
Brown paper
String

Line the cake tins with two layers of greaseproof paper by using the pencil to mark round the bottom of the tins, so that you have two pieces of paper which fit exactly into the bottom of each of the tins and then cut the paper to line the sides so that it rises above the edge of the tin by about 1 in to 1½ ins. Both layers of greaseproof paper should be oiled.

It is important that the greaseproof paper fits as smoothly as possible as any wrinkles in the paper will be repeated in the cake, which are difficult to cover with icing. Corners on a square cake need to be kept sharp as well. The best way to do this is to mark on the strips of paper which go round the side where the corners will come and then fold the paper firmly on these marks. When you stick the paper to the tin, or to the layer underneath, this will form a sharp corner. It is also a good idea to wrap two layers of brown paper round the outside of the tin, tied with string, to prevent burning.

THE BASIC MIX

Tin Size — Round / Square (quantities given as metric / imperial)

Ingredient	6 in R / 15 cm	5 in Sq / 13 cm	7 in R / 18 cm	6 in Sq / 15 cm	8 in R / 20 cm	7 in Sq / 18 cm	9 in R / 23 cm	8 in Sq / 20 cm	10 in R / 25½ cm	9 in Sq / 23 cm	11 in R / 28 cm	10 in Sq / 25½ cm	12 in R / 30½ cm	11 in Sq / 28 cm
1														
Plain flour	90 g / 3½ oz	75 g / 3 oz	150 g / 5 oz	100 g / 4 oz	200 g / 7 oz	175 g / 6 oz	250 g / 9 oz	225 g / 8 oz	300 g / 11 oz	250 g / 9 oz	400 g / 14 oz	350 g / 12 oz	450 g / 1 lb	400 g / 14 oz
Butter	75 g / 3 oz	50 g / 2 oz	100 g / 4 oz	75 g / 3 oz	175 g / 6 oz	115 g / 4½ oz	225 g / 8 oz	175 g / 6 oz	250 g / 9 oz	225 g / 8 oz	350 g / 12 oz	250 g / 9 oz	400 g / 14 oz	350 g / 12 oz
Soft brown sugar	75 g / 3 oz	50 g / 2 oz	100 g / 4 oz	75 g / 3 oz	175 g / 6 oz	115 g / 4½ oz	225 g / 8 oz	175 g / 6 oz	250 g / 9 oz	225 g / 8 oz	350 g / 12 oz	250 g / 9 oz	400 g / 14 oz	350 g / 12 oz
Ground almonds	25 g / 1 oz	25 g / 1 oz	25 g / 1 oz	25 g / 1 oz	50 g / 2 oz	25 g / 1 oz	50 g / 2 oz	50 g / 2 oz	65 g / 2½ oz	50 g / 2 oz	75 g / 3 oz	65 g / 2½ oz	90 g / 3½ oz	75 g / 3 oz
Black treacle	10 ml / ½ tbs	10 ml / ½ tbs	20 ml / 1 tbsp	10 ml / ½ tbs	20 ml / 1 tbsp	20 ml / 1 tbsp	30 ml / 1 tbsp	20 ml / 1 tbsp	40 ml / 2 tbsp	30 ml / 1 tbsp	40 ml / 2 tbsp	40 ml / 2 tbsp	60 ml / 3 tbsp	40 ml / 2 tbsp
Mixed spice	4 ml / ¾ tsp	4 ml / ¾ tsp	5 ml / 1 tsp	4 ml / ¾ tsp	7 ml / 1¼ tsp	5 ml / 1 tsp	9 ml / 1½ tsp	7 ml / 1¼ tsp	10 ml / 2 tsp	9 ml / 1½ tsp	15 ml / 3 tsp	10 ml / 2 tsp	20 ml / 3½ tsp	15 ml / 3 tsp
Brandy (optional)	10 ml / ½ tbsp	10 ml / ½ tbsp	15 ml / 1 tbsp	10 ml / ½ tbsp	18 ml / 1 tbsp	15 ml / 1 tbsp	25 ml / 1½ tbsp	18 ml / 1 tbsp	35 ml / 2 tbsp	25 ml / 1½ tbsp	35 ml / 2 tbsp	35 ml / 2 tbsp	45 ml / 2½ tbsp	35 ml / 2 tbsp
Eggs (size 3)	2	2	3	2	4	3	5	4	7	5	8	7	10	8
2														
Currants	150 g / 5 oz	75 g / 3 oz	200 g / 7 oz	150 g / 5 oz	275 g / 10 oz	200 g / 7 oz	375 g / 13 oz	275 g / 10 oz	450 g / 1 lb	375 g / 13 oz	500 g / 1 lb 2 oz	450 g / 1 lb	650 g / 1 lb 7 oz	500 g / 1 lb 2 oz
Sultanas	75 g / 3 oz	50 g / 2 oz	115 g / 4 oz	75 g / 3 oz	175 g / 6 oz	115 g / 4 oz	200 g / 7 oz	175 g / 6 oz	250 g / 9 oz	200 g / 7 oz	350 g / 12 oz	250 g / 9 oz	400 g / 14 oz	350 g / 12 oz
Glace cherries (cut up)	40 g / 1½ oz	40 g / 1½ oz	50 g / 2 oz	40 g / 1½ oz	75 g / 3 oz	50 g / 2 oz	90 g / 3½ oz	75 g / 3 oz	115 g / 4½ oz	90 g / 3½ oz	175 g / 6 oz	115 g / 4½ oz	200 g / 7 oz	175 g / 6 oz
Mixed cut peel	40 g / 1½ oz	40 g / 1½ oz	50 g / 2 oz	40 g / 1½ oz	75 g / 3 oz	50 g / 2 oz	90 g / 3½ oz	75 g / 3 oz	115 g / 4½ oz	90 g / 3½ oz	175 g / 6 oz	115 g / 4½ oz	200 g / 7 oz	175 g / 6 oz
Raisins	40 g / 1½ oz	40 g / 1½ oz	50 g / 2 oz	40 g / 1½ oz	75 g / 3 oz	50 g / 2 oz	90 g / 3½ oz	75 g / 3 oz	115 g / 4½ oz	90 g / 3½ oz	175 g / 6 oz	115 g / 4½ oz	200 g / 7 oz	175 g / 6 oz
+ Brandy	10 ml / ½ tbsp	10 ml / ½ tbsp	15 ml / 1 tbsp	10 ml / ½ tbsp	18 ml / 1 tbsp	15 ml / 1 tbsp	25 ml / 1½ tbsp	18 ml / 1 tbsp	35 ml / 2 tbsp	25 ml / 1½ tbsp	35 ml / 2 tbsp	35 ml / 2 tbsp	45 ml / 2½ tbsp	35 ml / 2 tbsp
Grated lemon and/or orange peel (optional)	4 ml / ¾ tsp	4 ml / ¾ tsp	5 ml / 1 tsp	4 ml / ¾ tsp	7 ml / 1½ tsp	5 ml / 1 tsp	10 ml / 2 tsp	7 ml / 1½ tsp	12 ml / 2½ tsp	10 ml / 2 tsp	15 ml / 3 tsp	12 ml / 2½ tsp	20 ml / 3½ tsp	15 ml / 3 tsp
Chopped nuts	40 g / 1½ oz	40 g / 1½ oz	50 g / 2 oz	40 g / 1½ oz	75 g / 3 oz	50 g / 2 oz	90 g / 3½ oz	75 g / 3 oz	115 g / 4½ oz	90 g / 3½ oz	175 g / 6 oz	115 g / 4½ oz	200 g / 7 oz	175 g / 6 oz

THE MIXTURE

Ingredients

RAISINS

The flavour of the brandy always enhances the cake better if the raisins are soaked in brandy overnight. If you do not have brandy, then sherry or a liqueur or even whisky can be used. Unless there is some religious or moral reason why alcohol should not be used in the cake, the cake always tastes better with some alcohol in it.

To soak the raisins, just weigh them out into a bowl (preferably with a lid) and pour the brandy over them during the early evening. During the evening give the bowl a gentle shake or turn the fruit over with a spoon, and cover it up again. By morning the raisins will have absorbed the brandy and be deliciously swollen and juicy.

Method of making the mixture

If you are making a three tier cake, then it is best to mix the quantities for the two top tiers together, and then the bottom tier separately (usually the two top tiers are equal in quantity to the bottom tier).

Put all the ingredients under (1) into a large mixing bowl and the 'dry' ingredients under (2) into another bowl and this is really the best way of going about it. Provided the margarine or butter is at room temperature, then either with a mixer or by hand the ingredients under (1) can be mixed together in one go. Make sure that the bowl you are mixing in is big enough to take all the fruit as well. If using an electric mixer to mix the ingredients (except the fruit, cherries and nuts) do not 'over-beat', as the cake will become too light, which will give you problems when stacking the tiers. For the same reason the flour must be plain and not self-raising. The brandied raisins and dried fruit (2) should be stirred in gently with a metal spoon and the nuts and cherries added last of all. An electric mixer is not really suitable for this process as it is too vigorous and would chop the fruit up.

Then put the mixture into the tin(s). Place tins in oven 140°C, 275°F, Gas Mark 1. Cover the tops with two or three layers of greaseproof paper resting on top of the greaseproof paper which emerges from the sides of the tin(s).

Test the smallest after two and a half hours. The larger sizes after three hours. This is usually done with a skewer, preferably a meat skewer, made of wood and when it comes out clean the cake is cooked. However, the method I prefer to use is 'listening' to the cake. If it is still making a faint 'bubbling' noise, a bit like lemonade fizzing, then the cake is not cooked and you should put it back in the oven for another half an hour or so. Providing that you do not forget about the cakes, at such a low temperature a cake is unlikely to burn, but an overcooked cake is much better than an undercooked cake. If after half an hour the cake is still 'fizzing', put it back in again and so on, until the cake is silent. The fizzing noise is caused by gases bubbling through moist mixture, so as long as that noise continues, the cake cannot be cooked.

N.B. If you are leaving out mixed peel, or any other fruit, then it is important that you add the 'missed out' quantity in another fruit, so that the total weight of fruit remains the same.

Never, ever turn a rich fruit cake out of its tin until it is cold. It is bound to break.

STORING THE CAKE

When the cake is perfectly cold (after about 24 hours) lay a large piece of foil across your working surface and place a couple of layers of greaseproof paper on top of it. Now turn the cake out upside-down onto the greaseproof paper. Leave the greaseproof in which the cake was baked on the cake, but peel off the bottom layers.

To 'Brandy' the cake

Pierce holes in the underside of the cake and slowly dribble a couple of tablespoons of Brandy over the bottom of the cake, then replace the greaseproof paper you have removed and carefully wrap the cake in the foil, taking care not to crease the foil, as pressure will reproduce the folds. Crumple the foil at either end to seal the package. Never store cakes on top of one another, nor with anything on top or underneath them as this can cause distortion of the shape of the cake. The cake can be made anything up to nine months before the wedding.

If you wish to you may 'brandy' the cake again about six weeks to three months before the wedding just to make sure that the flavour of the brandy is really present and that the cake is moist and succulent. However, do not be too generous with the brandy as it is possible to make a cake too moist and this, again, can cause 'toppling'.

To Glaze the cake
EQUIPMENT
(Cakeboards, 3 in wider than the cakes)
Saucepan
Pastry brush
Bowl
Sieve

INGREDIENTS
Apricot jam
When you have finished the keeping period of the cake and are ready to marzipan the cake, you must first 'glaze' the cake as this helps the marzipan to adhere to the cake surface and seals in the fats from the cake.

METHOD
1 To ensure that you have a flat cake to work on, turn the cake upside down. However, if it has risen during cooking, the top should be cut off, so that the cake will sit flat on the board, so that you have the bottom of the cake uppermost to work on, which should have good sharp edges and corners.

2 Make up a 'glue' of egg white and icing sugar and put some in the middle of each cake board and put the cakes on top of this. This will dry out and ensure that the cakes are firmly adhered to the boards.

3 Warm two or three tablespoons of apricot jam in a bowl in a saucepan which contains some water which is simmering. It is possible to obtain a special sieved apricot jam, but if you have to settle for an ordinary jam, then it must be sieved to remove the skins of the fruit which jam normally contains. Actually the cheaper the jam, the better it usually is for glazing.

4 When the jam is sieved reheat it and if necessary add a teaspoonful of warm water and stir into the jam until it is smooth, so that the jam is easy to brush into the cake.

5 Cover all of the cake with a fine layer of jam. Now you are ready to marzipan the cake.

To Marzipan the cake

The cake should be marzipanned not less than three weeks before the date of the wedding.

I would suggest that you buy your marzipan. It usually works out cheaper because ground almonds can be very expensive and, if they have been stored for some time, can be very difficult to work with. Marzipan can be bought well in advance and stored in a cool dry place (not the refrigerator). Check the label for ingredients if you are in any doubt as to whether it is a good make.

Marzipan should only consist of almonds, sugar and eggs and perhaps one other ingredient.

EQUIPMENT
Rolling pin
Small sharp knife
Cake stuck to board and recently glazed

INGREDIENTS
1800 g (4 lb) Marzipan (for three tier cake, 1125 g (2½ lb) for a two tier)
Icing Sugar

METHOD

1 Knead the marzipan together until it is pliable, doing each cake separately. Start with the largest cake first, this being the most difficult.

2 Sprinkle icing sugar on your surface and your rolling pin. Roll the marzipan out, turning the marzipan round occasionally to ensure that it is not sticking to the surface. If it does stick spread more icing sugar underneath.

3 Check that the marzipan is large enough to go fully over the cake by holding the cake and the board over the top. As the board is 3 in wider than the cake, this allows for the sides of the cake.

4 Now lift the marzipan on the rolling pin and fit one edge of the marzipan against one side of the cake.

5 Check that the middle of the cake and the middle of the marzipan are in line with one another and carefully lower the marzipan onto the cake, removing the rolling pin as you go.

6 Now with warm hands, mould the marzipan using quick, light hand movements, first rubbing across the top of the cake, then the top edges and then down the sides until the marzipan fully covers the cake, then trim off the remainder, very carefully, cutting into the corner where the cake meets the board.

Note: Although this is not the method generally taught in this country for marzipanning a cake, this is the way it is usually done in Australia and America.

I find this way much easier, less time consuming and much neater than trying to stick pieces round the side of a cake, with a large piece on top. So do try this method; if you take your time over doing it you should get a 'professional finish' on your first try!

DRYING OUT

The marzipan must now be left on the cake in the open air for, ideally, one week. Never ice on the same day as you have marzipanned. But in a real panic situation you can ice after 24 hours.

The longer you dry the marzipan out, the more certain you can be that stains will not come through onto the icing, but with the 'rolled out' icing you will find that we 'glaze' the marzipan again in order to get the icing to stick firmly to the cake and you will find also that this will effectively 'seal' the oils into the marzipan. However, it is preferable to leave the cake to stand for a week if possible.

Sealing

Sealing the marzipan is done in exactly the same way as glazing. Again, the whole cake must be covered in order to make sure that the icing will stick well and that there is no staining of the icing. You cannot 'seal' a cake which is to be iced with Royal Icing, as the apricot jam will 'rise' into the icing sugar and discolour it, so if you are Royal Icing, then you must leave the cake for seven days to dry out.

Flat Icing

ROLLED OUT ICING

This is the easiest icing in the world to do. It is not a boiled fondant icing and there is little which can go wrong with it. The taste when it is dry is the same as Royal Icing, but it will not go 'rock hard' – an advantage I have always thought.

EQUIPMENT

Scales
Bowl (small for liquid glucose)
Bowl (large for icing sugar – icing can be prepared in an electric mixer with a dough hook, but not with a beater, which can burn out the motor of the mixer. Only the biggest mixers with the dough hook should be used).
Spatula
Mixing Spoon
Table Spoon
Saucepan with simmering water
Rolling Pin

INGREDIENTS

for 1800 g (4 lb) which is enough for a 3 tier cake, 1125 g
(2½ lb) for a two tier
1800 g (4 lb) Icing Sugar
225 g (8 oz) Liquid Glucose (from chemist)
4 egg whites
Drop of blue food colouring (to whiten the icing)
Cornflour

METHOD

1   To weigh liquid glucose, heat the container in which it is held
    in the simmering water, so that it will pour easily. Put the
    bowl on top of your scales and zero the scales again, then
    pour sufficient liquid glucose into the bowl. This can be a bit
    of a sticky job, but do not give up, this is the most difficult
    part, once you have weighed out the liquid glucose, every-
    thing else is plain sailing.

2   Re-heat liquid glucose in the bowl in the simmering water.

3   Weigh out icing sugar and drop the egg whites into a 'well'
    in the middle.

4   Add the liquid glucose.

5   If you are using an electric mixer lower the dough hook into
    the middle of the icing sugar and turn onto the lowest speed,
    using the spatula to push the icing sugar from the sides of
    the bowl into the middle until it forms a ball. If there is
    insufficient liquid, add a little more egg white, but do this
    slowly, as the mixture should not be too wet.

6   If you are doing this 'by hand', then start off with a wooden
    spoon, mixing the icing into the middle and then use clean
    hands to form the 'ball'.

7   Turn the icing onto a working surface with plenty of icing
    sugar sprinkled over it and kneed it until it is cold (it might
    be a little warm due to the liquid glucose being warm) and
    even in texture.

8   Cover the place where you are going to roll the icing out well
    with cornflour (*not* icing sugar as this encourages it to stick)

The Cake

and roll the icing out carefully, as you did with the marzipan, checking that it is big enough to fit the cake as you go.

9 Make sure that your hands have plenty of cornflour on them before you start to 'mould' the icing to the cake as this gives a lovely silky finish.

10 Trim off any excess icing with a sharp knife. Rub any wrinkles or creases with your hands, covered in cornflour.

11 Leave the cakes to stand for about 24 hours.

Royal Icing

Royal icing can be used in large quantities to flat ice the wedding cake, if you are good at getting the icing flat, but other than this you will need Royal Icing to pipe the decoration onto the cake.

EQUIPMENT
Bowl
Wooden spoon
Sieve

INGREDIENTS
2 egg whites
450 g (1 lb) Icing Sugar

METHOD

1 Put egg whites in the bowl and 'break' them up with the wooden spoon, to break down the albumen, making sure that you do not beat them.

2 Add half the icing sugar and gently turn into the egg whites.

3 Cover this with a damp cloth (to prevent a crust from forming) and put to one side for about 20 minutes to half an hour to allow any bubbles to come to the surface.

4 Break any bubbles up.

5 Add the remaining icing sugar and stir in.

6 Beat the icing for about 20 minutes. It takes about 20 minutes to get the correct smooth stiff icing that will pipe well, without

being too thick. If after 20 minutes the spoon will not stand upright in the middle of the bowl, then add a little extra sugar slowly. If your arm starts to ache and you cannot get someone else to beat the icing for a few minutes, then cover it with a damp cloth and leave it until you feel your arm is strong enough again.

.N.B. Any icing which has to be left overnight should be covered with a damp cloth and placed in the refrigerator. The next morning it should be beaten again until it reaches room temperature and extra icing sugar added if it has gone too 'sloppy'. If the icing has formed a crust, it must be thrown away as if you break up a crust, the particles will block the icing nozzles and cause an uneven pattern.

Coloured Base Icing (Wedgwood effect)

Wedgwood effect need not only be done in blue. Pink, lemon, peach or any other colour can be used to match the Bridesmaids or any other colour scheme. If you are having your cake in a wedgwood effect it is better to match it to something, especially any table napkins, table flowers, etc. If you are using coloured icing to match the Bridesmaids' dresses, and if they have a polka dot pattern, then this can be easily reproduced in a pattern somewhere on the cake. If they have blue dresses with white sashes, then why not use wide white ribbon round each tier, to reflect the Bridesmaids' sashes. This is a simple way of decorating a cake with great effect.

Adding the Food Colouring

Only ever colour icing during daylight, never under artificial light as the artificial light tends to subtract from the colour.

Rolled out Icing

It is best to add the colour (a few drops, unless you know that the colour is weak – remember it is easier to add a little more colour later than to have to remake the icing because it is too dark) with the egg whites. Extra colours can be added during the kneading process if necessary, but do be sure that you have kneaded the colour through, otherwise the colour will give a 'marbled' effect.

Royal Icing

Colour should be added after the 20 minute beating process, and well beaten in to ensure even distribution of colour.

If you are colouring icing just for piping, never colour all the icing, always reserve a little plain white icing for sticking ribbon and decorations to the cake, as this will not show as much as with coloured icing.

Piping the cake

Jaconet or piping bags (as many as the colours you will want to use)
Adaptors (for the icing nozzles) (same number as bags)
Star Nozzle
No. 1 and No. 2 writing nozzles
N.B.   The above are much easier to use than the syringe type of icing sets, because the syringe relies on the pressure of the thumb only. With bags you can use your whole hand, or even two hands, if necessary.

Filling the Bag

Fit the adaptor and the nozzle you wish to use to the end of the bag, according to the manufacturer's instructions (small bags are the best). Turn the bag half inside out and put one or two 'wooden spoonfuls' of icing into the nozzle end of the bag. Then screw the bag firmly by lifting up the 'inside out' half and pinching the bag just above where the icing is and turning the rest of the bag firmly, then turn the screwed up part over to lay beside the half with the icing sugar in. This should keep the top part of the bag and your fingers clean.

Learning to Pipe

Stars and dots and lines are very easy to pipe and just a little practice will ensure a 'professional' finish. It is important if you are not used to icing to learn a few simple techniques well and to use these to good effect, rather than to try anything complicated. The patterns should be designed only to use simple lines, stars and dots, with advantageous use of inexpensive and easily bought decorations. Something like this done well will look much better than attempting a very difficult pattern, which might easily go wrong.

To pipe stars

Stars are very easy to pipe and make an attractive border for the top and bottom edges of a cake.

1 Hold the nozzle and the bag firmly about a quarter of an inch away from where you want the star. Hold the nozzle in one hand (left hand if you are right-handed) holding the bag itself in your right hand, so that your right hand is above your left.
2 Now squeeze gently with your right hand, maintaining an even pressure.
3 When the star is the size you want it, release the pressure from your right hand. If necessary take your right hand away altogether.
4 Then pull the nozzle away.
5 It is important that you have released the pressure before pulling away, otherwise you will get 'long' points to the stars, which will look uneven.

To pipe dots

These are done in the same way as the stars, but with a No. 2 or No. 1 writing nozzle, all depending on what size dots you require, No. 2 being the larger. If you are using a No. 1 nozzle, you may find it necessary to make the icing a little runnier, but try to pipe with normal consistency icing first, and if it makes your hands ache, then add a couple of drops of egg white.

To pipe lines

1   Put the nozzle close to the cake and start the line by squeezing gently.
2   Maintain the pressure evenly on the bag and pull the bag away from the surface you are icing and let the line 'drop' onto the surface. If you do not maintain an even pressure the line will break. Do not try to 'write' the line onto the cake as it will not give you a professional finish.
3   Again, to finish the line release the pressure in your hand and pull away.

Cornelli work

Cornelli work is a system of using wiggly lines to make a lace effect, which can be very pleasing to look at and is reasonably easy to do. It is a good way to fill an area, instead of lattice work, which is difficult to do unless you are practiced at it. Just let the icing fall onto the surface in lots of little curls and wiggles, making sure that none of the lines are parallel.

Decorations and their Uses

PLASTIC

Many of the traditional wedding symbols are available in plastic cake decorations and can be white or silver, namely horseshoes, doves, hearts, wishbones, cupids, wedding rings (these can be gold). The important thing with these is not too use too many different types and to create a pattern without overdoing it. For a three tier square cake twelve of one type of decoration and twelve of another is sufficient. This way you have one for each corner of the first type and one for each side of the second type. With round cakes, these are usually divided into six for the sake of decoration, and therefore multiples of six could be used.

RIBBON

Ribbon need not just be kept for the sides of the cake, but fine ribbon can be formed into loops to back a few flowers to go on the corners of the cake, with some ribbon loops included in a tiny vase of flowers on the top of the cake. This gives continuity to the cake. Flowers can be created out of ribbon as well, to decorate the cake.

FLOWERS (Silk)
Although fresh flowers can be used to decorate a cake, it is better to use them in a vase on the top to keep them looking fresh. To use them on the tiers of the cake is difficult without special little vases to sink into the cake and these can be hard to come by, so it is better to use silk flowers.

Silk flowers, the same as those carried by the Bride or her Bridesmaids, used to decorate the cake can be a cheap and very effective form of decoration. The small flowers could be used to decorate corners or sides, with a small group in the middle of each tier, whilst the larger flowers could be used in a vase on top of the cake.

This will automatically give the cake a sense of continuity and co-ordinate the cake with the rest of the wedding.

EDIBLES
Edible flowers can be bought in rice paper, icing sugar or marzipan. They can also be made by hand. It is not difficult to ice a rosebud. You need a small petal nozzle No. 18 (Tala) and a cocktail stick. First you form the bud round the cocktail stick standing the cocktail stick in some polystyrene. Make nine more in a similar fashion. Then return to the first bud and form two more petals round it, continue with the other nine rosebuds, replacing them all in the polystyrene. Then return to the first one and form three more petals round the outside. You then thread a small piece of wax paper over the unused end of the cocktail stick and gently lift the rosebud off the stick.

Cake tops
BOUGHT
There are available on the market, usually from stationers and

card shops, many wedding cake top decorations, some are even musical. Most of these feature a Bride and Groom.

The Bride and Groom may also be bought separately. From America there is also a range of cake decorations which feature cupids, doves, etc. When you buy these decorations, do not be frightened to add your own touches to them. With a plain Bride and Groom, you could always make a floral arch out of the same flowers as the posies. If you buy a Bride and Groom which is already in an arch, you can add a few coloured flowers or some ribbon in order to carry the colour right through the cake and make the top look more co-ordinated, especially if you are dressing your Bridesmaids in an unusual colour, such as lilac.

SILK FLOWERS

This area is covered under 'Floristry'. As previously mentioned flowers could be used in a silver or small cut glass vase, but when buying a vase, do remember that even on a three tier cake, only a tiny vase should be used.

Flowers can be used on their own, in a small posy, with ribbon or without, all depending on taste.

Use of Colour

When using colour on a cake, or in the flowers, or even the dresses, the colour must be carried through from the very top to the very bottom. This is why, if you are buying a decoration for the centre, you should add a touch of any colour which is in the cake to the top, even if it is just a tiny bow of ribbon.

Colour should be kept pale on the cake and should be used sparingly. Little spots of colour should be used as opposed to great 'blobs'. If you are in any doubt put a small amount of decoration on first and then add to it rather than putting on a lot and then trying to remove it because it looks heavy.

Odds and Ends

CAKE STAND AND KNIFE

A wedding cake never looks right, nor does any other cake for a formal occasion, unless it is on a cake stand. Bakers will usually hire their cake stand out, if they are not using it themselves on that day. If they are then some stationers, newsagents or card shops will hire them out. Catering hire companies also usually have cake stands for hire, together with the knife. The knife is important as well, as this is likely to feature in some of the photographs, and, of course, the cake does eventually have to be cut up. One thing that is frequently forgotten is a large knife suitable to cut up the wedding cake.

Cake stands can be bought, but as they are quite expensive, if they are to be used on one occasion only, then this would appear to be wasteful.

CAKE PILLARS

When you buy a cake, it is customary to return the cake pillars to whoever made the cake. Although some Brides feel reluctant to part with them, really there is very little use for cake pillars after the cake has been consumed, so it is normal to return these.

If you are making your own cake, you might ask your friends to see if they still have their pillars, as these are quite an expensive item and it would not detract from your cake in the least if you borrowed your pillars.

Cake pillars in this country usually come in silver or white plastic, or there are white chalk ones. I always feel that the plastic ones are more hygienic, although the chalk ones do look nice. However, the American ones which are available in this country are decorated with cupids and swans. These can have flowers added to them as well, so that you may carry your colour scheme right through the cake. Square pillars look best with square cakes, round with round cakes.

CAKE WITHOUT PILLARS

It is possible to design a cake without pillars. This is known as stack-on-stack. This is a very popular design in America and looks very Victorian. The main disadvantage is the lack of height, but it does save money on cake boards and pillars; you will have just as much cake and it is a more original style in this country.

All that you do to make a 'stack-on-stack' cake is to ice the bottom tier on a board and to ice the other two tiers onto a temporary board. When they are all set, you then stack the other two tiers onto the bottom one and then decorate them according to taste. The most popular form of decoration, which is very effective, is to have a garland of flowers sweeping down from the middle of the top tier in a spiral to the cake board, or even the stand, all depending on your preference.

Setting the Cake up

When setting your cake up at your reception, do try not to put the cake in the middle of the buffet table. It is preferable to find a good background, some curtains perhaps, and to set up a small table specially for the cake and flowers. Nothing looks worse than a wedding cake surrounded by sandwiches and wilting lettuce. If you are having your reception in a hall, it could be that there will be a stage and the cake could even be set up there. This will enable your photographer to get the best photographs of the bride and groom cutting the cake.

The same applies when there is to be a more formal wedding breakfast. If the cake is in front of the Bride and Groom, no one can see them during the meal, and all the guests are there to see the Bride and Groom. This also makes it very difficult for the Photographer to get good photographs of the Bride and Groom with their cake without them looking as though they are falling over, or as though they are trying to hide from him behind the cake.

CUTTING THE CAKE

The photographer will get the Bride and Groom to pose with their cake for photographs, pretending to cut it. Ideally the cake should be cut after the main course and the Best Man should announce that 'The Bride and Groom will now cut the cake'. If the Groom is in the Navy and owns a sword, this may be used to cut the cake.

The waitresses then remove the bottom tier of the cake, leaving the other two tiers standing, and cut this up in the kitchen, this is then served to the guests with their coffee, either in a personalised serviette or a cake bag so that they can save their cake if they wish to. It is considered bad luck for both the guest and the Bride and Groom if any guest does not take cake.

If it is not possible to cut the cake during the meal, because there is a buffet, then the cake should be cut at the beginning of the speeches. The cake can then be laid out on the buffet table for people to help themselves, but an announcement should be made that 'The cake is now available from the buffet table' with perhaps a mention of how it is unlucky for the Bride and Groom if any guest does not take a piece.

The Bride and Groom should cut themselves a slice and feed it to each other. Any remaining cake is put out for any guests who come to the evening reception or kept for sending out after the wedding.

CAKE BOXES
Cake boxes are available from most good stationers, newsagents or card shops and the Bride and Groom's name can be printed on them. These could be addressed to people who are not coming to the wedding before the wedding takes place if there is time available. If not, the Bride's mother can send the cake out on the Bride's behalf whilst she is on honeymoon, or the Bride can attend to this task on her return from honeymoon, maybe fitting it in with the writing of thank you letters.

'WITH COMPLIMENTS' CARDS
With Compliments cards can also be ordered from stationers to enclose with the cake.

THE CAKE

Confectioner (Baker) 1

Name _____   Two Tier £____

Address _____   Three Tier £____

Tel _____

Marks out of ten for quality and design _____

Confectioner (Baker) 2

Name _____   Two Tier £____

Address _____   Three Tier £____

Tel _____

Marks out of ten for quality and design _____

Confectioner (Baker) 3

Name _____   Two Tier £____

Address _____   Three tier £____

Marks out of ten for quality and design _____

Confectioner Decided on: Name and Address _____

Total Cost of Cake   £

Hire of Cake Stand and Knife   £

Cake Top   £

Total cost   £

Less Deposit paid   £

Balance due on _____ (date)   £____

COST OF MAKING IT MYSELF			
Ingredients	**Quantity**	**Price per lb**	**Total**
Flour			
Butter			
Sugar			
Ground almonds			
Black treacle			
Mixed spice			
Brandy			
Eggs			
Currants			
Sultanas			
Cherries			
Mixed peel			
Raisins			
Lemon/oranges			
Chopped nuts			
Marzipan			
Icing sugar			
Egg whites (whole eggs)			
Greaseproof paper			
Cake tins			
(hire or buy, if necessary)			
Hire of cake stand and knife			
Cost of silver decorations:			
Doves			
Horseshoes			
Bells			
Wishbones			
Shoes			
Cake top			
TOTAL			

Floristry

FLOWERS BY A FLORIST

When selecting a florist it is a good idea to wander round the shops and have a look at each Florist's window to see which style you prefer. Silk flowers look better and more realistic with plenty of leaves with them, so look for a florist who does this, if this is what you like. If you want fresh flowers, the silk flowers in the window will give you a guide, but you could get a better idea by visiting the florist on a Saturday morning (early) to have a look at the fresh flowers she will have waiting to go out. You could perhaps make advance arrangements with a florist to do this, giving the excuse that you have not got much idea of what you want and it would help you to see real flowers put together in a bouquet. If you want real flowers in your bouquet it is better to go to a florist, rather than to try to do them yourself as it can take years to learn how to wire flowers properly and to learn to select flowers which when prepared on the Friday night will be fresh on the Saturday morning. Also, apart from the fact that you are likely to lose a lot of sleep by having to stay up to do your bouquet (on busy Saturdays some florists stay up all Friday night preparing wedding flowers), if you do not like what you have done, then you will not have the time to re-make your bouquet, and quite probably the flowers will be too bruised and you will need new ones anyway, which can work out much more expensive than ordering them from a florist in the first place, as well as much more worrying.

It is a good idea to ring round the local florists to find out how much they would charge to make the bouquets or posies in your chosen shape, in order to get a price comparison and this should be done before you decide to do your own flowers, to make sure that you will actually be saving money by doing so. Generally speaking most florists, for example charge the same for a single carnation as they do for carnations made up into a buttonhole, for the obvious reason that they would rather make up the buttonholes than sell you the carnations cheaply, so do check up on this first of all, and it is easier to do this on the telephone in an anonymous fashion.

Delivery

COST

Most florists expect you to pay on delivery of the flowers, but do not charge extra for delivery, especially of wedding flowers, which is normally a large order.

TIMING

If you are going to a hairdresser's which is only a short distance from the Florist's then, perhaps, you could collect your flowers on return from the hairdresser, so that you know that you have them. However, if you are having your flowers delivered, ask for delivery early in the morning, about 10 a.m., this will save any last minute panic. Many Brides ask for delivery an hour before they are due to leave for the church/registry office, consequently the flowers have not arrived by the time the photographer turns up, thus delaying him. Also if the flowers are to be delivered late, and the florist has forgotten, then by the time you telephone it can be too late to do anything about it. Also bear in mind if your hair is being decorated with flowers that the flowers should be delivered before you go to the hairdressers.

If you are having the florist prepare silk flowers for your wedding, then there is no reason why you should not collect these a week or so before the date of the wedding and then if there is anything you do not like about them, you have time to ask the florist to change them.

KEEPING YOUR FLOWERS

When a florist makes up your bouquet, she will use very fresh flowers and will have allowed room for the buds to open, so they should not drop. However, if you are getting married on a very hot day in summer and for safety's sake you have had your flowers delivered in the morning and you are not to be married until 5.00 p.m., then some precautions can be taken to ensure freshness of your flowers. They should be kept out of bright sunlight in the coolest room in the house (if necessary, draw the curtains) and keep them damp with a water spray which gives a fine spray. These are quite cheap to buy. You could even ask the florist to deliver one with your flowers.

However, if finances will not permit this course of action, just very carefully sprinkle the flowers with small drops of water (large drops can 'bruise' the flowers). I do not advise people to put their fresh flowers in the refrigerator because if the temperature is too low, the flowers can become 'frostbitten'.

BUYING YOUR FLOWERS

Fresh Flowers

It is not really practicable for Brides or their mothers to make up all the bouquets with fresh flowers without previous experience of the wiring techniques and it takes florists years to gain the experience to wire flowers properly and to choose good stems in the first place. Making the bouquets either requires a very late night or a very early morning and with other duties to perform it is not a good idea to risk being tired. Also there is no sadder sight than a Bride walking up the aisle with a wilting bouquet, because the wiring has not been properly carried out.

However it is possible to make up fresh buttonholes. It is doubtful that these will work out any cheaper, but some Brides find satisfaction is doing this for their guests. The carnations should be bought on the day before the wedding and although the buds should be open, they should not be fully open. The stub wire is then pushed up the stalk of the carnation into the calyx, having been cut off at the first joint below the calyx. The wire is then left protruding to the desired length of the stalk, the fern is then attached to the back of the buttonhole with a little fuse wire and the stalk is then wrapped with the 'plastic' type of florist's tape.

Silk Flowers
WHERE TO BUY THEM

Most florists sell silk flowers together with their fresh flowers today, as do some departmental stores and I have even seen them in supermarkets and, believe it or not, petrol stations. There are also some specialist shops selling silk flowers only. Obviously the cheapest place to buy silk flowers is a wholesalers and these are usually found in the Yellow Pages under Florists' Sundries. However, many wholesalers will not deal directly with the public, although some will if the order comes to more than a certain amount.

The most important thing to do with silk flowers is to look at all that are available in your area, to check on the quality. Good quality silk flowers are only a matter of pennies dearer than the cheaper ones, but look a great deal better. Also by checking out all the sources, you can make sure that you are not paying too high a price for your flowers. Do be meticulous about pricing up, as this is a real opportunity to save money. Always make notes, never rely on your memory as to what the price of certain flowers is.

WHEN TO START WORK

You should start work on your flowers immediately you have an idea of what colour your Bridesmaids will be wearing. It may be a good idea to shop for your flowers on the same day as you purchase either the dresses or the fabric, so that you can take these with you for matching. If it is not possible to take the dresses with you, then take a sample of the fabric. If you are buying your dresses off the peg, trim just a little of the fabric out of one of the seams.

With silk flowers, the bouquets can be completed months in advance, and it is better to do this, as the last weeks before the wedding will be taken up with catering and finishing the cake. This will also ensure that you have plenty of time to reconstruct the posies if you are not satisfied with your first attempt.

Always make one of the Bridesmaids' posies first. If you have more than one to do, you can then copy the first one. This will have given you a little experience before you start the Bride's bouquet. You could start off with the buttonholes (if they are to be silk – a preserved form of asparagus fern is available which is imported from Italy), then work your way up to double button-holes, then the corsages, then the Bridesmaids' flowers, finishing up with the Bride's bouquet. never start the other way round as your technique will improve with experience.

Deciding on what is required

SHOWER

This is the 'teardrop' shaped bouquet. It may be long or short, closely formed or open in its construction. This is probably the most popular form of bridal bouquet. It is possible to have one large one for the Bride and smaller ones for the Bridesmaids.

CRESCENT

This is a small central posy with two points (which are 'mirror images' of each other), one either side. It is carried with the points downwards and can be used to echo the line of a crinoline.

WATERFALL

A bouquet with three points. There is a central posy with a long central point coming from it and two shorter points at the sides (mirror images of each other).

COLONIAL POSY

This is large circular posy of flowers, with no points. This is still a very popular form of bridal bouquet and goes very well with 'Victorian' style wedding dresses.

VICTORIAN POSY

This is a small circular bouquet, with a larger 'lace-back' behind it. These lace-backs are usually bought, but could be made from lace which has been included in the Bride or Bridesmaids' dresses.

It is not normal for this type of bouquet to be carried by the Bride, although it is occasionally seen, but is a very popular design for Bridesmaids. It is the most economical style of posy as far as flowers are concerned, the lace-backs being relatively inexpensive.

BASKETS

Although baskets are normally reserved for the smaller Bridesmaids, they can look equally effective for older Bridesmaids and the Bride as well. It can look very nice, especially if the Bride is wearing broderie anglaise or a 'peasant' style of wedding dress. The most popular type of basket is the 'Nell Gwynne', which is a flat basket and can be obtained in various sizes, to keep them in proportion to the Bride and her Bridesmaids.

PRAYER BOOKS

Prayer books are most popular for Bridesmaids and have a few flowers arranged on the top of them with a 'bookmark' of ribbon hanging from them. The bookmark may also have flowers attached to it, or even the flat type of silver cake decorations, horseshoes or bells, etc. Brides do occasionally carry a prayer book, particularly if there is an old one in the family. These are not usually white and therefore look best when the Bride is not in white. Generally speaking the prayer book can look a bit small and insignificant for a Bride and it adds very little colour to the Bride's outfit.

PARASOLS

Whenever a parasol is carried by a Bride or Bridesmaids, it is normal to have some flowers added to it, either in the form of a small posy hanging from the handle, or attached in a circle to the inside of the outer edge of the parasol. When the parasol is closed this will then form a bunch at the top, opening out into a splendid circle. It is necessary to sew on silk flowers for this latter form of decoration.

POM–POMS

Pom-poms are small balls of flowers and are probably the easiest of all the flowers to do. They are the most appropriate for the youngest of the Bridesmaids, with the next eldest carrying baskets, the older ones could carry Victorian posies and the Bride a shower bouquet. This would make life reasonably easy for anyone attempting to make up all the wedding flowers themselves.

Colour

MATCHING

It is best if something in the floristry matches the colour of the Bridesmaids' dresses, but with their bouquets mainly contrasting with their dresses – just a touch of the colour of their dresses is needed. The Bride's main flowers in her bouquet look nice if they match the Bridesmaids' dresses, with the rest of her bouquet in white or cream (depending on which colour she is wearing) and, perhaps a little contrast, e.g. if the Bridesmaids are in peach, then their main flowers would be say, white roses or carnations, with just a touch of, say, peach freesia, with white lily of the valley and stephanotis and white ribbon. The Bride would then carry peach roses or carnations (the flowers in her bouquet need not be the same as the Bridesmaids) with white freesia, lily of the valley and stephanotis. In the bouquet she would probably have white ribbon, although peach could be used, with peach and white ribbons hanging down at the back to give elegance.

TONING

Certain colours tone together well and it always worth investigating these. I give below some examples of colours which go together well. Generally speaking it is better to keep to no more than three colours (including white), that is to say white and two other colours, otherwise it can be difficult to evenly distribute the colour and this will give an uneven and 'blobby' effect.

Blue and yellow

Deep mauve and yellow

Pink and lilac

Pink and blue (although the contrast here is a bit severe)

Blue and lilac

Peach and white
Red and white

Experience shows that both red and peach look best with white on its own, although a little blue can be used with red and peach can be toned with pale yellow or even lilac.

Blue, yellow and pink all look striking with white on its own. However, lilac always looks better with a little pink added, or silk violets can add a touch of interest.

Using Your Colour Scheme

When choosing your flowers it is important that you think about your colour scheme very carefully before going out to order them. If your Bridesmaids are wearing peach, it is no use trying to introduce blue to the flowers, just because you see some blue flowers which you rather like. If you know that you are the sort of person who tends to do this, check out all the flowers first to see which flowers you prefer, before deciding on your Bridesmaids dresses. In this way you may get a better mental image of what everything will look like. Many Brides choose peach or pink for their Bridesmaids, when all their lives they have wanted to carry red roses at their wedding. If you are one of these people, think about this before you start. Red and pink can clash, but nothing like as badly as red and peach!

Which Flowers to Use Together

There are three types of flowers which you will need for each of the posies and bouquets – Large (focal) flowers, fill flowers and small flowers, i.e. large, medium and small.

LARGE FLOWERS

A bouquet always looks best with just one type of large flower, i.e. orchids, roses, carnations. These are the most popular. These flowers are the focal centre of the bouquet and all the other flowers are used to fill in between them, as are the leaves.

MEDIUM (FILL FLOWERS)

The fill flowers can be anything which is not one of the above. A bouquet of roses will not look right with rose buds interspersed amongst it. For one thing this would detract from the beauty of the roses. The fill flowers are kept slightly further back in the bouquet to draw attention to the focal flowers, hence these should either be white or a contrasting colour to the focal flowers. If you use the same colour flowers the bouquet will look just one heavy lump of colour. Fill flowers are usually small lilies, stephanotis, or freesia. Freesia can also stand on its own for a bouquet, especially if something colourful is required as all the natural colours, plus some fantasy colours are available in silk freesia. This can look very good in Bridesmaids' posies with lace backs.

SMALL FLOWERS

These flowers are used to give a delicate effect and stop the edge of the posy being too solid. As are the leaves. The usual flowers which are used are lily of the valley and Gypsophila. These also tend to shake slightly, giving a natural look. I never think that you can have too many of these flowers, provided they are used individually and carefully.

Corsages

These are the flowers worn by the two mothers and sometimes grandmothers have smaller ones, and even special aunts and godparents. A corsage is a large buttonhole containing two or three large flowers, with smaller flowers surrounding it, to give a more exotic effect. Ribbons can also be added. The most popular flower for the Bride's mother to wear is the orchid, although roses are still a popular choice. Carnations are rarely chosen as the other guests will be wearing them. Freesia is also an ongoing favourite. It is important to find out which colour everyone will be wearing, before choosing the flowers for the corsages, as these are so obvious and large, if they clash it is a disaster, and if they tone too closely, they will not show up; a pleasant contrast looks best. Where it is not possible to establish the colour of everyone's outfit, because they have left it too late to select one, then the best thing to do is to go for a neutral colour, e.g. cream (orchids in particular), white (not a good choice, due to the large amount of white at a wedding and everyone else wearing white buttonholes), pink (if you are absolutely sure no one is wearing orange!). The other alternative is mixed colours of freesia, which is both colourful and unlikely to clash with anything.

Buttonholes

GUESTS

Some Brides choose white buttonholes for the men and pink for the ladies, but this can be a wasteful and complicated way of providing buttonholes. If a lady is wearing a shade of red or orange, she will probably pick up a white buttonhole, some ladies do this anyway as many older women dislike pink. This will leave a lot of pink buttonholes over, with some men being left without a buttonhole. It would also seem inappropriate in this age of sexual equality. Also it can work out cheaper to buy 100 white carnations than 50 white and 50 pink. Any white carnations left over can be used in Bridesmaids' posies.

When thinking about numbers of buttonholes, most people think about one per guest, not counting the Bride, Groom, Best man, Bridesmaids and both sets of parents and anyone else who is having a corsage. However, it is possible to reduce the numbers of buttonholes necessary, by giving them only to members of the family, especially, when a lot of friends are invited to the Church. But if you decide to take this course of action, it is essential to ensure that the Ushers know each member of the family who is to have a buttonhole. It can be very embarrassing if a 'friend' is given a buttonhole, which leaves Great Aunt Ethel without one, especially if she is inclined to complain loudly about that sort of thing. I remember a family wedding which we were photographing, where I heard a guest complain loudly about the fact that the photographer had a buttonhole, when they did not! This was obviously bad manners on the part of the guest, but if you know that you have that sort of person coming to your wedding, then it is better if you give everyone a buttonhole.

GROOM, BEST MAN AND TWO FATHERS
The important men, namely the Groom, Best Man and the two fathers usually have double red carnation buttonholes, and these are made by carefully taping two single red carnations together with the fern. The Ushers are usually given single red carnations to distinguish them from other guests.

Some Brides, if they are carrying red roses, like the principal men to wear double red rose buds instead, with the Ushers and Page Boys wearing single ones. Where the men are in brown, especially if the Bride is carrying yellow roses, then yellow rosebuds might be considered more appropriate.

THE PAGE BOY
Traditionally the Page Boy should wear a pink rosebud, but many small boys will draw the line at wearing pink, and it is usually better to give them a red rose bud instead.

Table Flowers
Most Brides today feel that they would like their tables decorated with flowers and the cheapest way of doing this is to raid the garden. If you know well in advance when the wedding is to take

place, then the garden can even be planted not only to give colour in the photographs, but to yield flowers for the tables. Margarine tubs can be saved for containers, the tops being cut off. You can then fill the centres of these with Oasis foam and make up little posy bowls. If you do not have a lot of flowers, then use plenty of leaves. Three blooms per posy bowl with plenty of leaves will look pretty and you could use some ribbon as well to add a little colour.

If it is winter time and flowers are very expensive it is possible to make flowers from crepe paper or tissues to fill posy bowls, again using ribbons loops and plenty of evergreen foliage from gardens.

If this is not possible for a winter wedding, then you can beg and borrow specimen vases from friends, family and neighbours and buy a few daffodils, placing one with some daffodil leaves in each.

If you are making up posy bowls with flowers from your own garden, then these can be made up the day before the wedding. Never leave this job until the day of the wedding as it is quite time consuming.

Silk flowers can, of course, be used to make up table flower decorations, but the quantities required can be very expensive.

Cake Tops

WITH A VASE

Silk flowers can be wired together in a triangular pattern to match the Bride's flowers and any silk flowers used on the cake, and put in a small silver vase. If you are buying a vase, do consider the proportion of vase to cake. The vase must be minute, and with a two tier cake, smaller, or it will make the cake look top heavy.

If you are using fresh flowers, do not put water in the vase, because if the vase gets knocked, then the water may run all over the cake. The thing to do is to wet a little cottonwool and attach this with a rubber band to the ends of the stems of the flowers.

If the Bridesmaids are carrying Victorian posies, then it can look
very pleasing to make a small posy with tiny rosebuds to match
the Bridesmaids' posies for the top of the cake. You will have
to gather a little lace to form the lace-back, but the result can
look very good and this decoration is very inexpensive.

Another way is to take a small piece of Dri-Hard and to place
silk flowers in this to form a 'posy bowl' effect. You can then
let this dry and place on top of the cake on a piece of plastic
cut from a Margarine tub or yoghourt container, as the Dri-Hard
will mark the cake. Again do not forget to use some ribbon to
match that used in the bridal flowers. This ribbon can also be
used to trail down the sides of the cake, or just over the top tier.

Church Flowers

Most Churches will allow you to arrange the Church flowers
yourself if you like. Generally speaking there are flowers in most
Churches, but you can add to these if you wish.

If you are particularly good at flower arranging you may do
this yourself, or you can pay a florist or a floral artist you may
know to do this for you. Alternatively, you can ask the Rector
for the name of the person who usually handles the flower
arranging in Church and have a word with her as to how you
would like the flowers to look on your wedding day, finding out
what sort of quantities she will require and then buy the flowers,
allowing her to arrange them. If you want the ends of the pews
decorated then you should ask if the Church has the containers
for these. If they do not, then it can work out quite expensive
having to buy the containers.

Preparing the Silk Flowers

WIRING

There are two main designs of silk flowers. There are ones with
blooms which can be pulled off a stalk and some have a plastic
stalk, the top of which goes through the petals with the stamens

holding the blossom on (usually these are small flowers, e.g. gypsophila, violets).

With the former type, these are usually the larger flowers, roses, orchids, carnations, the blossoms and leaves are removed and the stalk discarded. You then take a lit candle and a wire stub (This is the florists' name for the wires used to strengthen these flowers. They need to be fairly thick.) and heat the end of the wire stub in the candle flame. The hot end is then inserted into the opening where the stalk was and placed against the plastic inside. Be careful not to pass this through too far as you could burn the polyester petals. The plastic then melts around the wire and you can be sure that it will not fall off. You do this to as many flowers as you will need.

For the second type, the individual flowers are cut off the central stalk, leaving plenty of stalk and the stub wire placed as high as possible beside the plastic stalk and the stub is taped to the stalk.

LILY OF THE VALLEY

Lily of the valley is usually found put together in fives and the individual stalks are pulled off the central stalk. At the end of each stalk will be a 'bulb' where the end of the stalk went over the end of the central stalk and this is cut off. The stub wire is then placed beside the stalk just short of the last two blossoms and the two are taped together.

TAPING

Any type of florist's tape can be used for silk flowers, although the Gutta tape can be difficult to use if you have no experience of working with it, as you need warm hands to finish it off. If you do not seal it properly it will come undone, which can be rather embarrassing. I have seen many people make this mistake, when making their own fresh buttonholes, so that everyone ends up with long green strands hanging down from their buttonholes.

Both the other types of tape, one is paper and the other plastic, are reasonably easy to use, although the paper is definitely the easiest of all and I strongly advise anyone unaccustomed to floristry to use this type of tape. With both the paper tape and the other plastic type of tape, you should stretch the tape as much as possible. This is both economical and gives a more delicate appearance to the back of the bouquets. The tape is then carefully wound round the stub, keeping the tape flat all the time. When putting flowers together the same method is used.

MAKING UP RIBBONS

I always find it advantageous to make up the ribbons before I start to make up the bouquets. Loops should be kept small and those to be included in the posies and bouquets should be of one or two loops. Three loops are only used if you are using a very narrow ($\frac{1}{4}$ in) ribbon, like picot. You can also leave points if you like. Points can look very good if they are all kept in the same direction, so leave very long points, these can be cut back later.

Ribbons for the top of the bouquet are usually made from wider ribbon (1 in or more). For a shower I make one three loop bow and one two loop. If I have used narrower ribbon in the bouquet I will make up the same in that ribbon as well. For a Colonial Posy I would make up five two loop ribbons or three of three loops.

These loops are made by deciding on what depth loop is required and making such a loop, it is held in that position with fuse wire. You then pass a stub up the middle of the loop and wind the wire round the stub, then cover the wire and the stub with tape. If you want double or triple loops, just form them in the same way and tie them with fuse wire, but you must tie them tight, so that they will not spring back.

Next you can make up any trailing ribbons you fancy, bearing in mind directions given under 'colour'. It is always better to make up too many as it is easy to cut out ribbons after the bouquet is finished, rather than to add them. The big loops for the top and the trailing ribbons are added to the bouquet at the end if it is a shower, so that the loops stand up at the back, covering the wires and the trailing ribbons hang straight down, or curled as desired. With the round posies, the long ribbons usually come out of the body of the posy, so that they look like a 'waterfall' gushing out of the middle of the flowers, especially with the Victorian posies. If you find it easier with the Colonial posies to let the ribbons hang down at the back, then this can be done.

LEAVES

The leaves are wired the same as the small flowers above. Make sure that you wire every leaf available.

DESIGN

There are a few basic rules which should be observed when designing bouquets which will avoid an amateurish appearance.

The first is never use four of anything anywhere, nor eight. Even if you are using six roses in a shower, make absolutely certain that you do not get four in a row, nor place the flowers in combinations of two, thus forming a four at the top.

This looks awkward and heavy. Large flowers should be offset to show the beauty of each flower.

The next most important point is about the points. Always use the smallest flowers in the points of any arrangement, with the flowers getting larger towards the centre of the design. This is so in showers and waterfalls and crescents, buds and small flowers should be used in the points, with medium-sized flowers further up and the large ones at the top.

With table arrangements, in a triangular display (usually the easiest for a novice to attempt) use buds and small flowers in the two further points at the bottom and at the top, with the larger flowers in the middle at the bottom. If you are in any doubt, practice with some of your silk flowers, before you make up the posies.

The third point is to carry the colour right through the design. That is to say if you are using a third colour, say, lilac with pink and white all three colours must be carried through the design evenly from the very tip of a shower to the top. This is why you are advised not to use more than three colours as with your leaves you will have four elements to include evenly in the bouquet. If you do not carry the colour through, the bouquet will look awkward and unbalanced. The carrying through includes the sides as well. If you keep a certain colour in the middle of the bouquet it will appear as a stripe and look rather ungainly.

Making up the Bouquets

SHOWER

First form the point, if you do this correctly, then the rest of the bouquet will look very good indeed. The best way I have found of forming a point is to use one stem of lily of the valley and a leaf, letting the lily overlap the leaf, then add one or two blossoms of your 'fill' flower, then a bud. Buds are essential where points are required. It is possible to buy a 'bush' silk rose, which is three different size roses on one stem and it is worth looking for these, they also have plenty of leaves on them. Now you can add another leaf and two sprigs of lily of the valley, with a piece more of your 'fill' flower and this time, say two buds and so on. Each of these is added to the central stalk. Place the flower where you think it would look best and then bend the stub to the central stalk. You continue in this way, adding more and more flowers until you get to the top and all your focal flowers are included and you have the length of bouquet that you want. Keep checking the bouquet to make sure that it all looks right. Remember, if your fill flowers are of a strong colour, lilac for example, to make sure that the stems of these flowers are shorter than those of your main flowers, ensuring that attention is drawn to the largest flowers. When you get to the top, 'fill' it in with your remaining flowers (you do not have to use all of them) and add your ribbon loops and your trailing ribbons and carefully cover the wires you have used to attach these with, with tape, and then cut off the stubs, so that they are all the same length and then use your tape to wrap the handle (be sure not to cut the wires too short) a number of times, so that no ends of the wires can be felt through it and then bend the handle down, to

QUANTITIES				
	Bride	**Adult Bridesmaid**	**Medium Bridesmaid**	**Small Bridesmaid**
	N.B. Small, medium and large in this part means small medium and large of the same type of flower, rose, orchid, etc. which should look alike and be of the same colour, if possible as the Bride's largest flower.			
Shower				
Large Flowers	6 large 3 buds	3 large 2 buds	3 large 2 buds	unsuitable
(Fill) Medium Flowers	12	7	5	
Small Flowers	12	7	5	
Lily of the valley	12 stems	7 stems	5 stems	
Colonial				
Large Flowers	6 large	6 medium	1 medium 5 small	6 small
(Fill) Medium flowers	12	5	5	5
Small Flowers	12	12	12	12
Lily of the Valley	12	9	9	9
Victorian				
Large Flowers	1 large 5 medium	1 medium 5 small	6 small	1 medium
(Fill) Medium	6	6	6	6
Small	6	6	6	6
Lily of the Valley	12	9	9	6
Waterfall				
Large	3 large 3 medium	1 large 3 medium	1 large	unsuitable
(Fill) Medium	12	12	12	
Small	12	12	12	
Lily of the valley	12	9	9	
Crescent				
Large Flowers	3 large 2 medium 2 buds	1 large 2 medium 2 buds	1 large 2 medium 2 buds	unsuitable
(Fill) Medium Flowers	12	9	9	
Small Flowers	12	12	12	
Lily of the Valley	12	9	9	

Quantities *continued*			
	Bride	**Adult Bridesmaid**	**Medium Bridesmaid**	**Small Bridesmaid**
---	---	---	---	---
Basket				
Large Flowers	6	5	3	2
Medium	12	12	12	12
Small	12	12	12	12
Lily of the Valley	12	9	9	6
(Ivy leaves also look very good trailing from baskets)				
Headdresses Small (in different colours, if necessary)	18	18	12	9

form a 'hook' to hook over the Bride's hand. So do not allow the handle to be too thick or heavy. 'Prune' the wires back if necessary, but not letting the handle become so light weight that it will not support the weight of the bouquet.

COLONIAL POSY

Colonial posies are formed by starting in the middle with one single flower, you can then add three leaves, three pieces of lily of the valley and three pieces of 'fill' flowers, you then place the other five of the focal flowers round this central piece, using your fill and small flowers together with lily of the valley evenly all round, then finish off with your ribbon loops (if you are using them) and any trailing ribbons.

The handle is not bent down with this bouquet, but make sure it is not so long that the Bride or Bridesmaid appears to be holding the flowers away from her. The handle should be about half an inch longer than the hand width of the person who is carrying it.

VICTORIAN POSY

This is made exactly the same way as the Colonial Posy, except that at the end, when you have added all the flowers, you must push the lace-back on. Make sure that the width of the flowers and leaves does not exceed the width of the lace-back. Both the Victorian Posy and the Colonial Posy look best if finished off with a row of leaves.

When you have put the lace-back on, push the stub with the trailing ribbons on through the lace-back from the front and then trim back the stubs to form a handle and wrap again, as above, but do not bend the handle down.

WATERFALL

First make the central point, then one of the side points, then make the last of the side points, bearing in mind that this must be a 'mirror image' of the first side point. Therefore, if you are making a pink/lilac/white combination, if there is a lilac flower on the left of the first side point, then one should also be on the right of the second point, otherwise it will not look even. When you have made these points, using the information given under 'Shower' (they should be about 4 in long for the middle one and 3 in each for the side ones), then you must make the central 'posy'. This is best made with three focal flowers, using leaves and lily of the valley to surround each one, with some fill flowers in the middle. You can then use this isosceles triangle with the point at the top to attach the centre point to. Make sure that this is firmly attached in the position that you want it. Now add the two side points and fill in round the top, with your 'fill' and small flowers and a little lily of the valley and add the ribbon loops and trailing ribbons to the handle and trim the stubs back. Now wrap the handle and bend it down.

CRESCENT

The crescent is formed in the same way as the 'waterfall', but only the side points are made. The handle is not bent down, but is kept short as with the Victorian posy, because in bending it down it would be visible from the front, which is rather unattractive. It is not normal to have trailing ribbons attached

154

to the back of this bouquet as there is not a central point for them to follow.

BASKET

To make a basket up so that it is secure and comfortable and easy to carry you will need 'Oasis-fix', Dri-foam and Dri-hard, as well as a plastic implement known as a 'frog'. This is a small square piece of plastic with four blunt prongs protruding from it. First you warm a small amount of 'Oasis-fix' in your hands and then push this firmly onto the bottom of the 'frog' and then push the frog firmly into the bottom of the basket, twisting it at the same time to gain extra adherence. Then take a piece of Dri-Hard and flatten it out like pastry and cover a small piece of Dri-foam with it, and push both together onto the frog. The reason for doing this is that Dri-foam is not strong enough to hold flowers in quantity in a basket because if the flowers get knocked they will easily come out. The Dri-foam is too heavy to be used in a lump on its own. Therefore, by doing it this way we get the best of both worlds, the strength of Dri-hard and the lightness of Dri-foam.

When you have done all this your flowers may be added. Put in some leaves first, then any darker or contrasting colour, then your main colour, then any lily of the valley.

Headdresses

It is very cheap to make headdresses yourself, but very time consuming as they tend to be rather 'fiddly'. The flowers used should be very small, large flowers and rose buds are too 'bulky', so it is better to use your 'fill' flowers or even smaller if they can be obtained in the correct colours. The smaller, the better. These flowers should be wired onto the finest wire available. Leaves should be used to give a natural look. The small Bridesmaids' headdresses at the Princess of Wales wedding wore Ophelia headdresses and everyone commented on the beauty of them. These are mainly made out of leaves, with just a few small flowers added. As your leaves come with your silk flowers anyway and are basically 'free', then plenty should be used.

For older Bridesmaids a single rose can be wired together with some lily of the valley and, perhaps a little ribbon, and this could be worn on one side of the head. If the Bridesmaid has a central parting, then one of these either side might look better.

For small Bridesmaids two or three small flowers can be wired together, with a very slightly larger one in the middle and this can then be attached to a plain hair-slide.

This method is ideal for small children with fine hair. Use plenty of leaves to cover the slide and to give you somewhere to use an extra couple of hairgrips, if necessary.

When making the 'halo' type headdresses, remember to leave small loops of fine wire, or perhaps to crochet a single chain and attach this to the inside of the headdress, so that you have somewhere to attach hairgrips.

Corsages

I always think it is better to treat corsages as small bouquets, rather than large button holes. If you are using large flowers, then a maximum of two should be used, especially with orchids and large roses. However, if the roses are not very big, then use two roses and a bud, the bud being used to form a point, with a leaf and little lily of the valley and the two roses can then be offset slightly with one slightly above the other. The spaces can then be filled with leaves, stephanotis, any other 'fill' flowers which form a pleasing colour combination, and, of course, lily of the valley.

Corsages can also be made up from freesia, either in a single colour, two colours or all the natural shades of freesia. With some silk freesia there is a bud on the stem and therefore a bud can be used to form the point, if not use a leaf and one flower, then add all the different colours evenly. It is better to choose say two of each colour, or, perhaps, three and then keep adding them in sequence, making sure that two of the same colour do not touch, if possible. Use leaves to help you with this.

NOTE ON RIBBONS

There are many different types of ribbon available on the market, but the best ribbon to buy is the Florists' ribbon or it is sometimes called 'paper' ribbon. This is very wide, but can be torn easily into two, four, six, however narrow you may require it, so that if you want large, wide ribbons for the Bride, but narrower ones for the Bridesmaids, then all you have to do is to split this ribbon down. As it is very cheap anyway, this makes this type of ribbon the most economical. This is also the ribbon that curls beautifully when drawn over the back of a pair of scissors. As it is so very cheap it is worth buying a complete reel of the same colour as the Bridesmaids, plus a reel of white, which can then also be used for decorating the cars, making table and church decorations, as well as decorating the fronts of the tables at the wedding reception and making other decorations for the hall.

There are other ribbons which are available like Decorette, which is a lacy ribbon and cannot be curled over scissors as it tends to tear, and picot is also popular as it is a double-sided satin ribbon with small loops along the edge which is very pretty but very expensive and would not be suitable for other decorations. Picot will not curl.

WEARING OF BUTTONHOLES AND CORSAGES

Gentlemen always wear their buttonhole on the left. Ladies should wear theirs on the right (although today, with sexual equality, many ladies prefer to wear theirs on the same side as the men). Gentlemen have the stalk of their flower pointing down, towards their shoes. Ladies have their buttonhole and corsage stalks pointing upwards, towards their hats!

TO PIN ON A BUTTONHOLE OR CORSAGE

Never poke a buttonhole into a buttonhole! It stretches the fabric and looks awful.

It is necessary for each person to have someone else to put their buttonhole on for them. Never use the small safety pins – they are difficult to use and do not hold the buttonhole firmly. *Use* pearl headed pins or dress makers pins with beads on (so that they will not pull through the cloth). Buy the longest ones available.

Starting from the back of the lapel (the part that lays against the jacket), pass the point of the pin through to the front of the lapel, to the left of the flower, which you will be holding with your left hand, the pin being in your right hand. The point of the pin then goes across the stalk just underneath the calyx and back through the fabric. The calyx is the fat, green lump holding the coloured petals of a flower. With fresh flowers, the pin can be pushed through the calyx. If the pin makes the lapel 'pucker', then bend the pin until the lapel lays flat. This looks neat and tidy.

With corsages the same system is followed, except that the pin is placed under the first flower nearest to the stalk. With some corsages, which are heavy, it may be necessary to use more than one pin.

PRICING
Flowers by a Florist

Florist 1 _____   **Florist 2** _____
Address _____   Address _____
Tel _____   Tel _____

Florist 3 _____
Address _____
Tel _____
(Give each florist marks out of ten for artistry)

	Florist 1		Florist 2		Florist 3	
	£	VAT	£	VAT	£	VAT
Bride's Bouquet (style)						
Bridesmaids						
Posy (Victorian)						
Posy (Colonial)						
Baskets						
Pom-poms						
Shower						
Waterfall						
Crescent						
Corsages						
Mothers						
Grandmothers						
Others						
Buttonholes						
Groom, Best Man						
Fathers						
Ushers						
Guests						
Presentation Flowers						
Table Flowers						
Cake top						
Church Flowers						

DOING IT MYSELF

	£	VAT

Bride's Bouquet

Large Flowers   No. _____ @ £_____ per _____

Medium Flowers   No. _____ @ £_____ per _____

Small Flowers   No. _____ @ £_____ per _____

Bridesmaids

Large Flowers   No. _____ @ £_____ per _____

Medium Flowers   No. _____ @ £_____ per _____

Small Flowers   No. _____ @ £_____ per _____

Extra leaves No. _____ @ £_____ per _____

Corsages

Mothers: Flowers   No. _____ @ £_____ per _____

Grandmothers: Flowers   No. _____ @ £_____ per _____

Others: Flowers   No. _____ × £_____ per _____

Buttonholes

Groom, Best Man

Fathers: Flowers   No. _____ @ £_____ per _____

Ushers: Flowers   No. _____ @ £_____ per _____

Table Flowers

Large Flowers   No. _____ @ £_____ per _____

Medium Flowers   No. _____ @ £_____ per _____

Small Flowers   No. _____ @ £_____ per _____

Church Flowers

Large Flowers   No. _____ @ £_____ per _____

Medium Flowers   No. _____ @ £_____ per _____

Small Flowers   No. _____ @ £_____ per _____

Presentation Flowers

Sundries

Wires   No. _____ @ £_____ per _____

Tape   No. _____ @ £_____ per _____

Ribbon   No. _____ @ £_____ per _____

Lace Backs   No. _____ @ £_____ per _____

Baskets   No. _____ @ £_____ per _____

Candles   No. _____ @ £_____ per _____

Total   £

Catering

HOTEL OR RESTAURANT

If you are intending to hold your wedding reception in an hotel or restaurant, then it is a good idea to write or telephone about three or four places to ask what facilities they can offer. You will need to know how many guests their function rooms hold, what the hire costs are, what sort of menus they can offer and the cost per head, and to see their wine list. You can then calculate your expenses and decide whether you want to have a formal wedding breakfast or a simpler, finger-fork buffet. Prices quoted usually include VAT and service, but do be careful to check this because these costs can add considerably to the final account. You may also require a changing room for the bride (sometimes you will find there is no extra charge for this.)

When you have selected the most attractive spot – many hotels have very pretty gardens, which are pleasant to use for a summer wedding – you should go along to sample the food and look at the surroundings before making arrangements.

On the following pages are suggested menus from an hotel, similar to those you might be offered.

161

BANQUET MENUS

The Burford Bridge Hotel
at the foot of Box Hill, Dorking, Surrey RH5 6BX
Telephone (0306) 884561

Menus by permission of Trust House Forte Ltd.
Prices on application to Terry Power, Manager

MENU SELECTOR

Starters

Egg Mayonnaise with crayfish

Chopped chicken liver-pate with
french toast

Potted Pigeon with crispy toast

Florida cocktail (fresh orange and
grapefruit segments)

Chilled melon with ginger wine sauce

Avocado vinaigrette

Smoked mackerel fillets with
horseradish sauce

Prawn and melon cocktail

Whole pear stuffed with cream cheese
and herb pate

Duck pate with pistachio nuts

Parma ham and Ogen melon

Artichoke heart in raspberry dressing

Avocado, mango cucumber lime sour
mayonnaise

Mango and prawn with fresh coconut

Half melon filled with mixed seafood
in brandy cream

Soups

Turkey and mushroom

Tomato and basil

Consomme with fresh vegetables

Leek and potato

Seafood with sorrel and Pernod

Turtle soup with cheese straws

Fish Course

Trout in hazelnuts and grapefruit
segments

Lemon Sole fillets stuffed in a lobster
sauce

Salmon trout in champagne sauce

Main Course

Casserole of chicken in red wine sauce

Breast of chicken Washington
bourbon and sweetcorn sauce

Loin of pork Westmorland, apricot
and lemon stuffing

Roast turkey Florida with pineapple
cherries in madeira sauce

Roast Norfolk turkey with chestnut
stuffing chipolata and cranberry sauce

Lamb cutlet reform (breaded cutlets
in spicy sauce)

Best end of English Lamb,
tomato and rosemary sauce

Duckling in Grand Marnier sauce

Crown of lamb with redcurrant jelly

Veal cutlet, mild green peppercorn
sauce

Roast rib of Aberdeen Angus beef,
Yorkshire pudding and horseradish
sauce

Escalop of veal Marsala

Roast Scotch Sirloin of beef,
pink peppercorn sauce

Saddle of veal Burford, pot roasted,
button onions, lardon bacon and
mushrooms

Scotch salmon butterfly in orange and
cream

Fillet of beef Wellington

Fillet of beef Perigodine,
madeira and truffle sauce

Vegetables

Potatoes: roast; croquette; duchesse;
parsley

Leaf spinach with cream

Buttered baby peas and carrots

Baby sprouts; Braised celery;
Cauliflower cheese; Buttered mixed
vegetables; Buttered peas

Whole green beans with almonds

Courgettes with tomato and herbs

Mixed salad; Green salad

Brocolli hollandaise
Bouquet of fresh vegetables

Desserts

Apple tart with whipped Jersey cream
Old English Sherry trifle
Lemon Water ice with blackcurrants
Poached pear with hot chocolate sauce
Profiteroles with chocolate sauce
Tropical fruit salad with whipped cream
Baked Alaska flambe
Iced blackcurrant souffle
Peach Escoffier, Whole peach in a
    brandy snap case coated with
    Kirsch flavoured sauce
Pineapple Aloha, Half baby pineapple
    filled with fruit and hazelnut ice
    cream

Iced Grand Marnier souffle
Jersey cream ices: Acacia honey with
    stem ginger; Woodland hazelnut;
    Fresh strawberry; Chocolate
Sorbets: Lemon, Pink champagne
Cheeseboard (always available as an
    alternative on request)

Coffee

Coffee with cream and petits fours

Speciality Menus

Victorian, English, Scottish, Lord
Nelson, Gala

In order to ensure prompt service and
piping hot food, please choose only one
dish per course.

Finger-Fork Buffets

FB1

Reception canapies
Sevruga caviar with oatmeal pancakes
Smoked Scottish salmon rolls
Asparagus roulade
Deep fried scampi
Miniature hamburgers with
    pepper sauce
Tartlets of curried prawns
Oysters baked with spinach
Bouchees of lobster and shrimp
Miniature pizza
Chicken sate
Bouchees of sweetbreads and
    mushrooms
Lamb cutlets, spicy sauce
Eggs stuffed with Danish caviar

FB2

Chicken livers in bacon
Cocktail sausages
Prawn and mushroom bouchees
Cheese and pineapple sticks
Salmon and shrimp bouchees
Finger sandwiches of egg
    and asparagus
Quiche of cheese and ham
Chicken bouchees
Goujons of lemon sole
Hot fried scampi
Rolls of rare roast beef in aspic
Deep fried mushrooms
Smoked salmon whirls

FB3

Quiche of cheese and ham
Smoked salmon whirls
Goujons of lemon sole
Prawn and mushroom bouchees
Finger sandwiches of egg mayonnaise
Chicken livers in bacon
Reception sandwiches of baked Ham
Cocktail sausages
Thin cucumber sandwiches

*Buffet prices are shown on the menu
selector. You may wish to consider
adding a sweet and coffee from the
menu selector.

With the exception of FB3 the above
may only be prepared for over thirty
guests.

Ideally your booking should be placed immediately after booking the church or registry office and you will probably be expected to pay a deposit of about 10% to 30% per head and the balance about fourteen days before the date of the reception. It is not generally a good idea to choose an hotel or restaurant which is miles from the place where the ceremony is being held, and you should make sure non-drivers have transport provided, and that everyone is given a map of how to get there.

ADVANTAGES

The main advantage is that everything is done for you and all facilities will be at your disposal.

DISADVANTAGES

This really is an expensive way of entertaining your guests. The bill for drinks alone is likely to be very heavy, and the food and drink will carry a service charge and VAT. It is still safer to allow a contingency fee of 20%, and if you really are working to a budget make sure that the hotel or restaurant are aware of how much you intend to spend and that you do not wish to over-run this amount. Work this all out well in advance and get it confirmed in writing.

Formal Wedding Breakfast

A Wedding Breakfast is so called from the time when marriages took place early in the morning followed by a Mass. In those days the Church dictated that no food should be taken prior to taking the Communion bread and therefore the meal following the wedding was 'breaking the fast'. Today, however, with most weddings taking place in the afternoon the Wedding Breakfast has come to mean the food served after the wedding ceremony, which is usually closer to tea time or dinner time, and the 'formal' part means to sit down and have the meal served by waitresses.

DRINK

It is usual to greet your guests at the reception with a glass of sherry, or another aperitif, and to serve wine with the food, but an economy can be made by providing wine from the start right through to the toast when Champagne is usually served. White wine is best for a buffet, but red wine should be served with red meat or game.

If you are providing an open bar for your guests and wish to limit the cost, then arrange to set aside a certain amount for this after which guests will be expected to pay for their own drinks. Close contact should be kept with the hotel management to arrange seating plans and table decoration.

AT HOME

ADVANTAGES

The advantage of having the Reception at home is that it is less expensive and saves having to ferry the food to a strange place, perhaps some miles away, where, if anything has been forgotten it can mean a long, time-consuming run home. A wedding reception at home means that the whole thing is obviously more homely and probably more comfortable than it would be in a hall.

DISADVANTAGES

The main disadvantage is lack of space. Unless you have a really large house you will have to prune your guest list to the minimum.

Thirty is a comfortable number to entertain for the average household. Obviously if it is a warm sunny day, then the garden can be used, but it is difficult to count on such weather even in high summer, in this country.

Also, it means that you will have the extra work of tidying the house before leaving for the Church or Registry office and after the wedding reception there will be a great deal of cleaning up to do.

MARQUEES

ADVANTAGES

Marquees overcome the problem of lack of space at home and some quite large ones can be erected in quite small gardens, meaning that the problem of the weather does not arise.

DISADVANTAGES

If you are having a large number of people to the reception, it may be decided that a caterer is needed and the caterer will wish to use your kitchen. The same problem of the house being tidy still arises and although you may anticipate that the guests will stay in the Marquee, they will probably need to trail through the house in order to use the toilet, which brings up another problem. With, more than fifty or sixty guests, even an upstairs and downstairs toilet will be insufficient.

Marquees are also fairly expensive and usually cost about the same as hiring a hall.

HALLS

ADVANTAGES

Halls are reasonably priced and enable you to do your own catering and normally to supply your own drink, although this is not necessarily the case. Generally speaking, the halls are cleaned beforehand by the caretaker and the hirer is only expected to tidy the hall and sweep the floor after the reception.

DISADVANTAGES

Disadvantages are that they can be a fair distance from the Bride's home, requiring a great deal of running about on the morning of the wedding, especially if something is forgotten.

Some local authorities have appointed caterers who have the right to, sell all drink consumed on the premises or to charge corkage. This includes the wine as well, so that if you want to serve wine with the meal, the Council's Caterer can ask you to pay them money for each bottle of wine that you open, which can work out very expensive, so it is worth checking up on this first.

In cold weather public halls can be very cold, and they are sometimes inclined to be a bit 'grubby'.

You will also find that you are restricted to time. Most public halls have to be vacated by midnight, or even 11.30 p.m. Access can also be limited, or if the hall is required all day if you are doing your own catering, then there can be extra charges for that. Some Local Authorities also make an extra charge if you wish to use their kitchen.

	£	VAT

HOTEL RECEPTION CHARGES

Hotel 1
Name
Address
Tel:
Contact:
Room Hire
No. of Guests
Cost per head
Aperitifs
Wine
Champagne
Overnight accommodation
Changing accommodation
Changing Room for Bride
Service Charge
Total £

Hotel 2
Name
Address
Tel:
Contact:
Room Hire
No. of Guests
Cost per Head
Aperitifs
Wine
Champagne
Overnight accommodation
Changing Room for Bride
Service Charge
Total £

Hotel 3
Name
Address
Tel:
Contact:
Room Hire
No. of Guests
Cost per Head
Aperitifs
Wine
Champagne
Overnight Accommodation
Changing Room for Bride
Service Charge
Total £

Hotel Chosen:
Name:
Address:
Tel:
Contact:
Menu Agreed:
Room Hire:
Cost per Head:
Aperitifs:
Wine:
Champagne:
Overnight Accommodation:
Changing Room for Bride:
Service Charge:
Total Cost:
VAT

TOTAL   £
Less Deposit   £
Balance due   £
on _____ (date)

HIRING A CATERER

If you decide to hire a caterer choosing which one to employ is probably the most difficult decision you will have to make. Unless you are recommended to one, the first thing you should do is to look through the Yellow Pages and local papers under 'Caterers' and 'Wedding Services', and telephone each one and ask them to send you menus. When you have the menus you can then compare prices, but this can be very misleading as the prices do not give an indication of quantity or quality and it does not necessarily follow that the most expensive will give the best service. If a caterer is registered in the Yellow Pages, then because of the way the Yellow Pages take their advertisements, you can be sure that they have been in business for at least a couple of years whereas a Caterer advertising in the local press may have started his business that very same day.

Check all the menus through very carefully and look for hidden extras like 'linen'. Some caterers only price up the food, but do not include in these prices things like the linen, china or service. Some will include in their pricing the cost of the provision of disposable table linen, plates and cutlery, but will charge extra if you want china. Value Added Tax is normally an extra so look very carefully to check whether VAT is included or excluded.

VAT Registration is one way of knowing that a caterer has been in business for some time and does a certain amount of business each year, and you have to be good to stay in business, but there are many good companies who cater on a part-time basis and are not, therefore, VAT Registered and this will give you an advantage from the point of view of cost.

Basically you will only get what you pay for. I would say that you need menus from a minimum of six caterers. Discard the most expensive and any whose prices are a great deal less than the others. Then investigate more fully. Find out if any of your friends has heard of them and whether they were satisfied. Interview each caterer individually. Most caterers are prepared to go to a client's home in the evening to discuss the matter.

Catering

When employing a caterer it is also important to find out what is the maximum number of guests they are accustomed to catering for and to check whether they are familiar with the hall and the facilities that you are hiring for the occasion. It may well be that although they can quote you for providing hot food, the kitchen facilities are inadequate for serving that sort of meal in large numbers. If your caterer does not know the hall, then make arrangements to meet him there before accepting the quotation, so that you can be assured that if they need to bring in extra large equipment for cooking and keeping the food hot, there is sufficient accommodation for it.

If the caterer does not feel confident to provide the sort of meal you want in the hall you are proposing to hire, then it may be necessary either to try another caterer, or look at another hall, or even restrict your numbers or choose a different menu. This requires a great deal of consideration, which is why you need to think about the catering well in advance and not to book everything firmly until details are settled to your entire satisfaction.

When you are fully satisfied that you are going to get good value for money, pay your deposit. Most caterers expect the bill to be fully settled either in advance of the wedding or on the same day in cash. Make sure you are aware of these details before booking. Some caterers take up to one-third of the value of the contract as a deposit, which is usually non-returnable, so make absolutely sure that you really do want his services, because if you cancel you will lose a lot of money.

Beware of ladies trying to earn 'pin-money' through catering, although a few are very good, they are not usually geared up to deal with a large wedding and you will not get the professional finish that you are looking for and you will probably not pay a lot less than hiring a fully professional caterer.

SELF CATERING

Formal Wedding Breakfast

ADVANTAGES

This is a more disciplined way of organizing your guests. If you are able to employ reliable waiting staff then you are able to relax and enjoy the meal knowing that you will only be needed in the background to keep an eye on things and to make sure that everything runs smoothly. There is no doubt that this kind of reception will be a lot less expensive than one held in an hotel or restaurant.

DISADVANTAGES

It can be difficult to get waiting staff, unless friends can recommend helpers to you. It is therefore likely that virtual strangers will be employed, so unless you are positive that you are hiring really efficient waiting staff, then careful checks should be made to ensure that it would not be cheaper to allow professional caters to handle the whole thing in the first place.

BUFFETS

ADVANTAGES

It is extremely easy to lay out a buffet table and to just cover the guests' tables with tablecloths and to let them help themselves. A choice can be offered (which is difficult to do with a formal wedding breakfast), although this can be expensive and wasteful. It is not necessary to hire good staff for this, except to do the washing up if you are not using disposable plates.

DISADVANTAGES

At a large wedding, where there are one hundred or more guests to be served, it can take a great deal of time for everyone to serve themselves and sit down, so that the last ones to collect their main course will have been overtaken by the guests who were first who will probably have finished their dessert by this time. It can also be very disorganised, with no one knowing where they should sit. Also buffet food does tend to look rather unappetising after a short while, as people take portion after portion from each dish.

It should also be borne in mind that the food will have been laid out fairly early in the morning and it will be necessary to take precautions during hot or stormy weather to keep this covered and cool.

The Final Solution!

So what, you ask, can you do if you want to do everything yourself and have a well organised wedding, without employing staff to help you? Well, it is quite easy to combine the very best aspects of a formal wedding breakfast with the best aspects of a buffet and make life very easy for yourself and your guests. In the morning when you are setting out your tables take a plate for each guest and on it put a serving of cold meat, fish, pastries etc. which they may be having. Lay the tables in exactly the same way as you would for a formal wedding breakfast, with cutlery, glasses, napkins etc., together with place cards and a formal seating plan. Then cling-wrap each plate (this can be disposable or china, all depending on your preference) and put this in each guest's place. Salads could be served similarly on small side plates. The dessert on a plate or in a dish should be placed at the top left, wine glass to the right. The salads, pickles, cream for the dessert are placed in bowls with spoons or servers which are placed at regular intervals down the middle of the table. I usually allow a bowl of everything to every six people (if you have a large selection of salads and pickles, then it could be one to every eight. In this way you can be sure that your guests have a seat when they arrive and new and accustomed people to talk to. You will be able to sit down and enjoy the wedding reception (and rest your feet!). Everyone should finish eating together, so that the speeches can proceed. It is ideal if you can arrange for a couple of people to make the coffee in large jugs and to serve it to the guests. Milk and sugar could be set out earlier when you initially lay your tables, or handed round by your assistants. If you do have someone to make the coffee, it is useful if they can then clear and wash-up, and then everyone will get a chance to enjoy the meal and the reception and this, after all, is the point of it all!

EVENING BUFFET

It is not necessary to think about an evening buffet unless you are having a disco or a dance in the evening. This can be extremely expensive – unless you have some arrangement where guests pay for their own drinks, like the reception being held in an hotel or restaurant or pub, so that you can put a set amount of money behind the bar, so that you can buy your guests their first drink or two, after which they pay for their own drinks.

So very careful consideration should be given as to whether it is desirable to continue the festivities on into the evening as this will double the cost of the wedding. If you do decide to carry on into the evening, as your guests will probably have had their wedding breakfast at 5.00 p.m. (this is about usual for a 3.00 p.m wedding), then it is customary to give the guests something extra to eat during the evening in the form of a 'finger buffet'. This means anything that the guests can pick up with their fingers. Although you would provide plates, most guests prefer to help themselves to bits and pieces when they want and to carry on with the party. This light refreshment should be served at about 9.00 p.m. to coincide with the return of the photographs (if these are coming back that evening). This gives the guests a chance to stop and look at the photographs, and at this point the music is toned down to 'background music', the serving of the buffet is announced, together with the arrival of the photographs and the lights put on for half an hour or so.

It is not a good idea to start putting out lots of salad or food which is difficult to eat whilst talking or dancing – it should be the sort of food which requires no effort to eat or handle and savoury food rather than sweet.

Catering

Menus

Hot

It is not really practical for a Bride and her mother to organise hot food to be served to a large number of guests, because most of the preparation would, of necessity, have to take place at the very same time as the actual wedding is taking place in church. However, for guidance when dealing with caterers, hotels, restaurants, etc., we give a few suitable menus. Hot food is really only desirable in the winter and even then, if you serve three courses one of them can be cold.

Menu A	Menu B	Menu C
Minestrone Soup	Grapefruit Cocktail	Prawn Cocktail
Roll and butter		
Hot Roast Beef	Hot Roast Turkey & Stuffing	Hot Roast Chicken
Roast Potatoes	Hot sliced Ham	Roast Potatoes
Boiled Potatoes	Boiled Potatoes	Chipolata Sausages
Peas	Peas	Peas
Sliced Green Beans	Sliced Green Beans	Sliced Green Beans
Fruit Salad	Hot Apple Pie	Fresh Cream Gateaux
Cream	Cream	Cream

Cold

Menu A	Menu B	Menu C
Prawn Cocktail	Grapefruit Cocktail	Egg Mayonnaise
Cold Sliced Turkey	Cold Sliced Ham	Cold Sliced Beef
Cold Sliced Ham	Hard Boiled Eggs	Savoury Flan
Cocktail Sausages	Sausage Rolls	(Quiche Lorraine)
Green Salad	Green Salad	Green Salad
Coleslaw Salad	Coleslaw Salad	Coleslaw Salad
Potato Salad	Potato Salad	Potato Salad
Roll and butter	Roll and butter	Beetroot
		Roll and butter
Fresh Cream Gateaux	Trifle	Fruit Salad
	Cream	Cream

It is easier to purchase cold meats ready cooked from the delicatessen counter of your local Supermarket, this is not only cheaper, but it also avoids too much work for anyone who is doing the catering themselves. For a large number of people it is very time consuming to have to cook a number of turkeys or joints of beef and this would have to be done the day before the wedding, which can be tiring and if anything goes wrong can leave you with a lot of problems, which could prove expensive to correct.

COMBINATION

It is assumed that if you are having a formal 'sit down' type of reception, that you will have staff and therefore if you wanted to give your guests some hot food, either because the weather is cold or because you have a preference for hot food, then instead of a cold starter you could give your guests soup. If you really want a quick and easy way out you could use packet soup (from a Caterers' pack), which is easily made up. However, you must remember that you will need very large containers to make soup for a lot of people and you should check on the size of the cooker(s) available at your reception hall to ensure that you will be able to do this on the cooker.

You could also give them hot potatoes instead of the potato salad. It would be very difficult for your staff to peel and cook sufficient boiled potatoes for, say a hundred guests, so a reasonable alternative is the tinned New Potatoes, which are also available from wholesalers in large tins. These only need warming through and most people like these, especially if they are provided with butter pats to melt over their potatoes. These could be put on the table in bowls with small bowls of butter pats either side, together with servers, so that guests can help themselves.

It is not necessary for the waitresses to serve each individual guest as this is time consuming and will require a large number of waitresses, which is expensive. The staff could also make up complete salads in the kitchen and just serve these complete to the guests. This, again, saves time and staff, and the food can be made to look very presentable.

Buffets
HELP YOURSELF

If it is not possible to arrange the 'sit down' type of buffet suggested earlier and you have to allow people to help themselves, it will probably be because you are having your reception at home and there is not space to lay the tables out, and this will probably mean that there are not so many guests. However, if possible, you should at least lay a table for the principal Bridal party, the Bride, Groom, Best Man and both sets of parents and the Bridesmaids as well. If the Bride and Groom sit down, this will encourage the guests to do so, so that everyone is seated when you are ready for the speeches. When you are holding your reception at home during the summer, if the weather is good, your guests could sit in the garden. Set the food out indoors, but put chairs and tables in the garden and people can wander out if they want to.

For a serve yourself buffet a wide variety of food can be offered, but bear in mind, though, that the greater the variety you offer, the more expensive and the more time consuming it becomes. If you wish to offer a selection we give some idea below of what should not be too time consuming to organise. Remember, though, you do not allow one portion of everything for each guest.

Menu A	Menu B
Cold Turkey	Egg Mayonnaise Sandwiches
Cold Ham	Ham Sandwiches
Quiche Lorraine	Turkey Sandwiches
Sausage Rolls	Sausage Rolls
Green Salad	Veal and Ham Pie
Coleslaw Salad	Quiche Lorraine
French Bread and butter	Coleslaw Salad
Cheese Boards	Pickles
Gateaux and cream	Trifle

'Sit Down' Buffet

For a 'Sit Down' Buffet a special kind of menu is required as it has to be arranged so that some of the food can be put on the tables in bowls, but not too much otherwise there will not be sufficient room to put all the food out, so that when you come to lay your tables and find out everything will not fit neatly onto the tables, a crisis arises. If you find that this is the case and for any reason there is not sufficient room to put everything on the tables, then, make up each guest a salad the way the cafeterias do and cling wrap this and put one in each guest's place. This can still look very nice, especially if there is plenty of colour. If you are in any doubt about space in the first place, it may be better to decide to take this course of action anyway. We specify below how much you would allow for each guest.

Menu A

Cold Sliced Norfolk Turkey	(½ slice)
Cold Sliced Ham	(1 slice)
Hard Boiled Egg	(½ egg + teaspoon of mayonnaise)
Sausage roll	(1)
Lettuce	(one leaf shredded)
Cucumber	(four slices)
Onion Rings	(four)
Beetroot	(2 slices)
Coleslaw Salad	(1 tablespoonful)
Potato Salad	(1 tablespoonful)
Grated Carrot	(2 teaspoonsful – this is good for colour)
Roll and butter	(1 roll and 1 butter pat each)
Gateau	(one sixteenth of a large gateau)

Menu B

Cold Sliced Ham	(1 slice)
Quiche Lorraine	(one eighth of 7″ tin, one sixteenth if larger)
Hard Boiled Egg	(½ egg + 1 teaspoon mayonnaise)
Prawns	(2 teaspoonsful of frozen, peeled, 2 fresh unpeeled prawns)
Salads	As above
Roll and butter	(1 roll and 1 butter pat each)
Trifles	(make these up in paper trifle cups, or wine glasses, and give each guest one).

Menu C

Cold Roast Beef	(2 half slices)
Sausage rolls	(1)
Veal and Ham Pie	(small finger of pie)
Hard Boiled Egg	(as above)
Roll and butter	(1 roll and 1 butter pat per guest)
Salads	(as above)
Strawberry Flan and cream	(one sixteenth of large flan, one eighth of small one)

If you wish to give your guests pickles, then you can still put these down the middle of the table in small bowls, because the vinegar can taint the rest of the food on the plate.

We would warn you about putting the salad on the plates in

advance, if you are using paper plates, as the coleslaw dressing tends to make these go soggy.

CHAMPAGNE RECEPTION

A champagne reception is a particularly nice way of celebrating a wedding and keeping the reception short. It would be easy for the Bride and her mother to arrange themselves and is ideal for, say 50–60 guests, where the Bride and Groom are getting married either in the morning or early afternoon and wish to get away during the afternoon.

It is not necessary to actually provide champagne any good white wine will suffice like a Veuve du Vernay or even Asti Spumante. Chilled Liebfraumilch is very acceptable too. This is a really lovely way to entertain your guests where you have a nice garden and it is a warm sunny day. It will, under these circumstances, be a wedding, which everyone will remember.

The food is kept simple, but luxurious. You are not intending to give your guests a meal, as such, but a few snacks and you need not, therefore concentrate on making sure that they are full up. Thus your aim is quality, not quantity. One of everything should be allowed for each guest.

Menu A
Smoked Salmon Sandwiches (on brown bread, crusts cut off) ($\frac{1}{2}$ round per guest)
Prawn Mayonnaise Vol au Vents
Sausage rolls
Crab canapés
Stuffed eggs (boiled eggs with yolks removed and mashed with mayonnaise,
a little curry powder, salt and pepper and placed back in the whites. Allow
$\frac{1}{2}$ egg per guest)
Cucumber sandwiches ($\frac{1}{2}$ round per guest)
Large Mediterranean King Prawns
Fresh strawberries and cream (or any other fresh fruit in season)

Menu B
Egg Mayonnaise Sandwiches (on brown bread)
Ham Sandwiches
Cucumber Sandwiches
Sausage Rolls
Cheese and Ham Vol au Vents
Stuffed Eggs
Fresh Fruit Salad and cream

Menu C (for winter)
Hot pasties (bought from the Supermarket and warmed in the oven)
Baked potatoes in their jackets with grated cheese
Sausage rolls (could be heated through)
Mushroom Vol au Vents
Stuffed Eggs
Ham Sandwiches
Salmon Sandwiches
Sherry Trifle and cream

With the winter menu, especially if the reception is for only twenty to thirty guests, then it might be rather nice to give your guests mulled wine instead of chilled white wine.

With a Champagne reception the guests are given wine on arrival and not sherry as with the other types of reception.

AFTERNOON TEA

If you are to be married at about 1.00 p.m and then you and a few guests are going to a restaurant for a lunch after the ceremony, then you may wish to bring them back home with you whilst you change, to see you off on your honeymoon. This most usually occurs after registry office weddings. In such circumstances, as the guests have already had a good lunch you may want to give them just a little to eat in the form of afternoon tea: a few small sandwiches with the crusts cut off and some small cakes, preferably fresh cream ones, should be served with a cup of tea. Possibly prior to this you may have given your guests a glass of wine each. The serving of the 'tea' would give the Bride and Groom time to change and they would join their guests with a cup of tea before leaving on honeymoon. The wedding cake could be cut up and served to the guests at this time, particularly if it was not possible to take the cake to the restaurant or because you wished to keep the lunch a small private affair.

EVENING BUFFETS

As previously mentioned it is not worth putting out a great deal of rich, sweet or complicated food in the evening. It should really only be a small amount of food for each guest. You could even have your staff prepare individual disposable plates with a 'ploughman's supper' on (i.e. French bread, butter, cheese, pickle and pickled onion, and a little salad) and have these handed round to guests. This is desirable if space is limited and a large number of guests are expected as it saves having to lay out a buffet table. The ploughman's supper could be handed across at the bar.

Menu

Sandwiches – Ham
Cheese
Egg
Salmon
Sausage rolls
Fingers of Veal and Ham pie
Quiche Lorraine (cut into fingers)
Crisps
Nuts
Pickles (onions and gherkins)

If you have paid caterers to provide the wedding breakfast for you, it is possible that they will insist on catering for the evening buffet also, although this is rare unless you are holding your reception at a restaurant or hotel. I always think that it is reasonably easy for the mother of the Bride (and the mother of the Groom if they feel they would like to work together) to prepare the Evening Buffet in the interest of saving money.

Recipes and Presentation

SALADS

Coleslaw Salad
1 white cabbage (sufficient for 40 guests)
450 g (1 lb) carrots
225 g (½ lb) onions
100 ml (6 tbsp) mayonnaise
20 ml (1 tbsp) lemon juice or wine vinegar
20 ml (1 tbsp) sugar
salt and pepper

Shred the cabbage finely. Grate the carrot. Chop the onion into small pieces. Mix together. Mix mayonnaise together with remaining ingredients. (Alternatively you can buy coleslaw dressing. Pour this over the cabbage mixture and toss well together. This can be made the day before the wedding.

Rice Salad

This is a very colourful and easy to make salad. Like coleslaw it is cheap to make and is filling and tasty. It can be used as a substitute for potato salad or in addition to other salads mentioned.

450 g (1 lb) patna or basmati rice (basmati has a better flavour, but tends to be rather expensive)
2 packets of Stir and Fry Mediterranean Style (or one fresh chopped onion, 2 red peppers, 2 green peppers, and a tin of sweet-corn niblets)
100 g (4 oz) sultanas

Boil the rice in plenty of water. If you are using ordinary domestic saucepans you will need two or three saucepans. Add the raw rice to cold water with some salt and bring to the boil. Allow the rice to boil for about 12 minutes and then lift out one grain and bite through it. When there is no gritty feel as you bite through the rice, then it is cooked. If the rice starts to absorb all the water, just add more water. When the rice is cooked, drain it in a strainer and run under cold water. Allow the strainer to stand over the empty saucepan so that the rice can drain well. When the rice is quite cold tip it into a bowl and add the remaining ingredients. More Stir and Fry can be added if desired or more dried fruit.

This salad can be made the day before the wedding.

POTATO SALAD

Cold Boiled New Potatoes
Onions
Frozen peas (cooked briefly)
Mayonnaise or Salad Cream

The potatoes may be freshly cooked at home, or taken from a tin, whichever is easiest for you. Again, if there are a large number of guests, preparing and cooking such a large quantity of potatoes could prove a mountainous task, if so it is better to buy the tinned or packed potato salad either from the supermarket or wholesaler.

Cut the potatoes up into pieces, but do not try to make them into little cubes like the canning companies do. The rough chunks shows that it is homemade and guests like this. Chop the onions finely and add one onion to 2 lb of cooked potato, together with a handful of cooked frozen peas and pour over the mayonnaise. This salad can be made the day before the wedding.

GREEN SALAD

Green salad is the name given to all the green and white vegetables used in a salad, like lettuce, cucumber, onion, celery, watercress. You will find the quantites you will need of these vegetables listed under 'Quantities'. It is not necessary to provide tomatoes, but they are of course very colourful, and you could, if you wish cut a few into quarters to decorate with.

You can make up bowls of green salad if you wish by chopping up all the ingredients and mixing them in the bowl with some French dressing, or the green salad can be put on the plate with the meat. This does tend to make the plate look more interesting. This then means that you only need bowls of coleslaw and potato salad and rice salad, with small bowls of pickles, which is much cheaper on the hireage. Remember if you have one hundred guests and three salad bowls between six, you will need fifty salad bowls. If this still proves too expensive and you are hiring china plates for all your guests, then it is best to have all their salad put on their plates.

Simple Starters

EGG MAYONNAISE

Egg Mayonnaise is a very cheap and easy starter to prepare, and it looks attractive too.

1 egg per guest
5 ml (1 tsp) of mayonnaise per egg (4 tsp = 1 tbsp)
A little lemon juice
Shredded lettuce
Paprika pepper

First hard-boil the eggs. This can be done two or even three days before the wedding. On the day of the wedding add some lemon-juice to the mayonnaise so that it is of pouring consistency (or you could use salad cream, but mayonnaise definitely tastes best.) Place a little lettuce on each plate (side plate size). Halve the eggs lengthwise and place yolk down on the lettuce. Pour the mayonnaise over each one and garnish with a little Paprika pepper.

PRAWN COCKTAIL
Prawns (allow a 450 g (1 lb) pack of peeled frozen prawns to 15 guests)
Lettuce
Mayonnaise (1 teaspoon per guest)
Tomato Purée
Little lemon juice
Cayenne Pepper

Prawn cocktail can be served on flat plates, in sundae dishes or in wine goblets (glasses). Take the prawns out of the freezer in the morning for an afternoon wedding, or the evening before for a morning wedding. Shred the lettuce and put a little in the bottom of each container and place a few prawns on top. Mix the mayonnaise with the lemon juice so that it will pour (this is not normally necessary for salad cream) and add a little tomato purée just to colour the sauce and a dash of cayenne to flavour it. Taste this to make sure that you like the flavour and then pour over the prawns. You can garnish this with a half a slice of lemon if you wish (from off-licences, designed to be put in gin and tonics – cutting lemons up is time consuming and expensive.) Brown bread and butter should be placed on the side plate.

GRAPEFRUIT COCKTAIL

Grapefruit cocktail is the easiest of all the starters to make up. It is best to use tinned grapefruit as this is sweeter and guests tend to prefer it. It is very time consuming for you to have to cut up grapefruits and to cut round each one inside the skin. Also many guests find it embarrassing trying to wrestle with a grapefruit and squirting their neighbour in the eye with the juice, so tinned grapefruit really is best.

Many Brides are against having grapefruit as a starter as it is not very filling, but you could always give your guests potatoes and rice salad to follow, as grapefruit can be very refreshing on a hot summer's day. To make grapefruit cocktails just put about a tablespoon of grapefruit into each glass cover with juice and add half a cherry to each one, for the sake of colour and presentation.

MEAT

We do not advise that you start cooking your own meat. This is, again, very time consuming and can work out very expensive. It is better to go to your local Delicatessen counter and order the number of slices of roast beef, turkey or ham or whatever you require. In this way you get good neat slices and exactly the amount you require. Remember to order the number of slices and not weight.

DESSERTS

With desserts the same advice follows as with everything else: do not complicate your life by trying to cook everything fresh yourself. Fresh cream gateaux are reasonably priced at most freezer centres and over the years of our experience, we have never found a way of making these gateaux as well and as cheaply as the manufacturers.

If you want to make flans, then buy the bases. These are quite inexpensive. You can then use two tins of fruit per large flan case, or provide fruit from your garden, if you grow soft fruit. By using whatever fruit is in season you could cut your costs tremendously. Should you have time, it might be possible to take advantage of 'Pick Your Own' offers from local farms, which should be done two days before the wedding. The flans are then filled the day before the wedding. For trifles, there are very good caterer's packs, in which you do not even have to cook the custard. However, if you cannot get hold of these use trifle sponges, a tin of fruit and a jelly for each one and get to this stage with your trifle two days before the wedding, if you like. Then either on the day before the wedding, or in the early morning of the wedding either make your custard or use the variety that does not need cooking. You could even get your staff (if you have some) to do this for you. All you need to do then is to add a few glace cherries for decoration, or some coconut. It is best not to pipe fresh cream, especially during the summer, as it will go buttery during the day. It is preferable to hand pouring cream round in jugs, or to obtain individual portion controlled pots of cream from the wholesalers.

CATERERS' SUPPLIES

A number of items have been mentioned above which can only be obtained from wholesalers. Other things which may be useful are portion controlled salt and pepper (in little straws), portion controlled sugar, and little individual tubs of salad cream. All of which can be put on the guest's side plate. If you cannot obtain a wholesaler's card, then you may be able to obtain some of these items through your local grocer who may be able to get these for you from the wholesaler, adding on a little extra profit for himself. Sometimes freezer centres stock some of these items, but if not, they may also be prepared to obtain them for you, at a small cost, especially the independent ones.

Quantities

Item	Quantity	Per no. Guests	
Cabbage Lettuce	1	10	
Webbs or Iceberg Lettuce	1	20	
Caterers' Tin of Grapefruit	1	15	
" Tin of Potatoes	1	15	
Tin of Fruit Salad	1	15	
Onions	450 g (1 lb)	25	
Coleslaw (see recipe)	1 Recipe	40	
Box of Coleslaw (Caterers' Pack)	1	25	
Box of Potato Salad (Caterers' pack)	1	25	
Rice Salad	1 recipe	40	
Ham (best to order no. of slices)	450 g (1 lb)	8	given as
Turkey (best to order no. of slices)	450 g (1 lb)	8	a guide for
Beef (best to order no. of slices)	450 g (1 lb)	8	pricing up.
Caterers' Trifle Packs	1	25	
Whole chickens	1	4	
Pie filling (for flans) in Caterers' size tin	1	5 flans	
Flans	1 flan	16 guests	
Prawns – peeled and frozen	450 g (1 lb)	15	
Beetroot – large catering jar	1	50	
After Dinner Mints – Caterers' pack	1	75 mints	
Wine	1 bottle	6 glasses	
Sherry	1 bottle	12 glasses	
Champagne	1 bottle	6 glasses	
Spirits (Whisky, Vodka, Gin, Brandy, Bacardi, dark rum, Pernod)	1 bottle	36 tots	
Beer	3 pints	per man	

Stocking the Bar

It is difficult to judge the amount of beer required but it is safe to allow 3 pints of beer per man. Many of our clients say 'Surely this cannot be enough', but it must be borne in mind that guests will be driving and aware of the danger to themselves and their families if they drink too much and drive. Consequently, over the past few years, the amount of drink consumed has dropped considerably. Brown Ale and Guinness are not very popular drinks and you can buy a six pack of each of these as well if you know someone particularly drinks them. Then take about one tenth of the quantity in light ales in half pint cans.

About one third of the remainder should be bitter and the remaining beer should be lager. Lager is very popular, especially in high summer. Although you could go half and half with the bitter and lager.

We would like to make a very serious point about barrels at this stage. Many clients order barrels and taps from off licences as this appears to be a cheap way of buying beer. However, it can be very wasteful. If you start on a particular barrel, the off licence will not normally take the barrel back, so even if one pint has gone from it, the remaining 29 pints have to be thrown away. Whereas, if you have cans, whatever is left over can be kept for another occasion.

SPIRITS

For the spirits we allow 1 bottle of scotch and 1 bottle of bacardi (which seems to be popular with the young) per 50 guests. Of the remaining spirits we allow 1 bottle per 75 guests. You can round up or down as your finances allow.

150 GUESTS IN THE EVENING
25 pints of light ale in half pints
100 pints bitter
100 pints lager
3 bottles Whisky
3 bottles Bacardi
2 bottles Vodka
2 bottles Gin

2 bottles Brandy
2 bottles Pernod
} Although these are not strictly necessary, if you supply them, you will need these quantities, to make sure that they last the evening out.

1 bottle Dark Rum (optional)
Lemonade – 36 litre bottles
Cola – 36 litre bottles

188

Catering

American Ginger Ale –12 litre bottles
Tonic – 2 litre bottles
Fruit juices – Orange, Pineapple, Tomato, Grapefruit – 3 cartons
of each.

This should give you plenty of drink for everyone, but if
there are other drinks, like babycham, and aperitifs you can
add them. Cinzano Bianco is a popular drink as is sweet Martini.
Very few people seem to drink the Dry, unless it is mixed with
gin. We would advise 1½ litres of Bianco and Sweet Martini per
100 guests.

Hiring

FURNITURE

If you are holding your reception at a hall, you will find that
they have tables and chairs there, but do check to ensure that
there are sufficient. If there are not or if your reception is to be
held at home in a marquee or just in the garden, you may find
you are short of tables and chairs and these can be hired from
hire companies, who are sometimes found under 'Tent Hire' in
the Yellow Pages.

TABLEWARE

The first thing you have to work out is what cutlery is needed.
One of each of the following will be needed for each guest.

Cutlery

Starter	Teaspoon	Prawn cocktail, grapefruit cocktail
	Soup Spoon	Soup
	Knife and Fork	Egg Mayonnaise
Main Course	Knife	
	Fork	
	Small Knife	
Dessert	Dessert Spoon and fork	Gateau, flan, apple pie, etc.
	Tea spoon	Trifle in trifle cups or anything in sundae dish
Coffee	Coffee spoon	

China

Starter	Sundae dish	Prawn cocktail, grapefruit cocktail
	Soup bowl	Soup
	Side plate	Egg Mayonnaise

Main Course	Dinner Plate	
	Side plate	
Dessert	Sundae dish	Fruit cocktail, trifle
	Dessert plate	Gateau, flan, pie
Coffee	Coffee Cup and saucer	

Glasses

Sherry	Sherry glass (a wine glass could be used, if necessary, but you will not have time to wash these up and use them for wine, so a double quantity will be required.)
Wine	Paris goblets (wine glasses)
Champagne	Champagne flutes. If you are serving wine with the meal and champagne separately for the toast, then extra glasses will be required. Again, wine glasses can still be used for champagne. The important thing is that the glass is narrower at the top than at its widest part, to keep the bubbles in.

SERVING DISHES, ETC.

If you are putting the salads straight onto the plates as we suggest, you will not require any serving dishes and this can make quite a saving. If you want to put the salads on the table, however, you could borrow bowls and dishes from friends and neighbours, but do ask them to mark everything clearly as to whom it belongs, otherwise you will be left with the onerous task of sorting everything out and this has been known to take years. The main disadvantage of this is that it is doubtful whether anything will match.

COFFEE

There are two ways of dealing with the coffee, one is to put the cups and saucers on the table and give instructions for your staff, or whoever is arranging the catering to make up a number of coffee pots full of coffee and for them to put these on the table with milk jugs and sugar bowls. This requires extra hireage, which can, again, be quite expensive. It is more economical if you have a couple of staff in the kitchen to leave the cups in the kitchen. The staff then make up the cups of coffee (if instant coffee this can be put into each cup before the wedding, so that the hot water just has to be poured over it) and hand them round to the guests.

Catering

TEA URN

It is possible to hire a tea urn, or a Baby Burco from most hire companies and this is an essential piece of equipment. It allows large amounts of hot water to be heated reasonably quickly. This hot water is not only used for the tea and coffee, but also for washing up (many halls have indadequate methods of supplying sufficient hot water to wash up large quantities of crockery, cutlery and glass), and for heating tinned potatoes. With tinned potatoes, boiling water poured over the potatoes which are left in their own tins, with the original liquid drained off, is sufficient to heat them, if left to stand for a while. This saves having to hire large saucepans. You may also need hot water to make up packet soups, if you are having this.

OPTICS AND GLASSES

Optics are automatic measures which can be attached to bottles, used mainly in public houses, but they can be hired for special occasions like weddings. If you are running your own bar, then we feel that a great economy can be made by hiring these. It saves guests being given over measures, and your drink from disappearing too quickly. Most off licences, if you buy your drink from them, will loan you the glasses and the optic measures, or make a nominal charge for both. If you are buying your drink from the Off Licence week by week, which a lot of people do, explain to the off licence that you are doing this and ask if he will lend the glasses. If he will not, then approach another off licence. If you are buying your wine and champagne from him, ask for the wine and champagne glasses as well.

CAKE STAND

Do not forget to hire a cake stand from a stationers, the bakers or the hire company. Alternatively, someone good at carpentry can make a rough stand, which will go under the table cloth, to give the cake extra lift.

Tableware

PLATES

There are three types of disposable plates, paper, card (microwave) and plastic. The paper plates are very cheap, but tend to go soggy if anything wet like vinegar or salad cream comes into contact with them. The Microwave and Chinette plates are made from stiff card, which has been coated and they are reasonably priced. These will not go soggy and are a good alternative to paper. They are also very attractive. The plastic plates work out more expensive to buy per plate, than to hire china, but are re-usable.

CUPS AND GLASSES

There are plastic glasses available on the market, but very few people seem to enjoy a drink from one of these and if you can borrow your glasses at no extra charge from the off licence then there is little point in buying them.

Paper cups are only for cold drinks and it is a good idea to get some of these for children to use, even if you are hiring china and glass. Nothing can ruin a wedding quicker than a child being seriously injured by a broken glass. Polystyrene cups can be bought for hot drinks. However, few people enjoy a cup of tea from these. You should first check in the hall to see if there are any cups and saucers which you could use, and if not, even if you are using disposable plates, consider hiring cups and saucers for the coffee. It really does add a finishing touch.

CUTLERY

If you do not wish to hire cutlery, plastic cutlery is reasonably cheap and is easily available on the open market. It can be washed up and used again. An advantage is that you can drop it into a plastic bag and wash it up the next day. However I must stress that it is not very managable, and does on occasion break.

Catering

Storage of Food

FREEZERS

Freezers can be very useful when preparing for a large wedding. Cakes and gateaux can be bought or made well in advance (about a month), but remember you cannot freeze jellies, cooked pastry (you can, but it tastes like cardboard afterwards), quiches (there is a definite loss of quality with freezing). You can freeze sausage rolls, but not if you are making them with frozen pastry or frozen sausage meat, as they would need cooking before freezing and sausage rolls, like all pastries, loose quality when cooked and frozen. It is better to buy the ready made frozen ones.

Sandwiches can be frozen, provided they do not contain boiled egg, mayonnaise, salad cream or any salad vegetables. These should be made up just a week or less before the wedding and frozen.

REFRIGERATION

Bearing in mind that most of the preparation is going to take place one to two days before the wedding, a large amount of refrigerator space is going to be required and if you do have access to a fridge belonging to a friend or neighbour it could be very useful.

You should make arrangements for delivery or collection of the meat, which being already sliced, will require no preparation, either as late as possible the day before the wedding or even on the morning of the wedding itself.

The salad can be collected late on the day before the wedding. Lettuce can be kept fresh by cutting all the leaves off and placing them in cold water overnight. The next morning the water is drained off and the lettuce placed in a large plastic bag (disposal bag if you like) and this is knotted. The lettuce will then only require rinsing, drying and shredding on the wedding day. To wash your lettuce use washing up bowls, clean buckets etc. These can be left in the garage overnight, or even in the garden (provided there is no frost and they are covered with a weight on top, to protect them from animals).

Keeping the wine cool

It is possible to buy from camping shops blocks which can be frozen in the normal way, which when removed from the freezer stay frozen for a long time. These can then be packed into boxes with the wine to keep it cool.

The staff or a couple of the parents will then open the wine whilst the guests are drinking their sherry and place the bottles on the tables. You may need some help to open the champagne bottles as champagne has to be served immediately or it will go flat.

Ice Cubes

Plenty of ice cubes can be made over the month before the wedding and should be accumulated in a large plastic bag in the freezer. The more ice cubes you make, the more they will keep each other frozen, when removed from the freezer.

On the day of the wedding take the plastic bag out of the freezer as late as possible and place it in a brown paper bag (if possible) or a box and pack it round with plenty of newspaper, remembering to pack plenty of newspaper underneath as well. When you have finished with your frozen blocks, these can be placed on top as well as more newspaper. This is only necessary when you are hiring a hall because they never have freezer facilities. Obviously if you live near the hall, then you could return home to get your ice cubes, but they still need insulating well, because the hall will get very warm during the evening and one ice bucket full of ice is nowhere near enough for a hundred guests.

SERVING THE SHERRY

If you are hiring staff, then they can stand at the door with trays of sherry. If for reasons of economy you decide to buy only one type of sherry it is better to get a good sherry, so that everyone has one glass each, rather than a lot of cheap sherry. Your guests will really notice the difference.

If you are not hiring waitresses, set out the sherry glasses on a table near the door (these should be filled). This can be done in the late morning. Cover the glasses with a cloth, remove the cover and hand these out to the guests as they arrive.

The Tables

TABLE LINEN
HIRING

Most catering companies hire out tablecloths in white demask, which you will have to wash before you return them. This can work out quite expensive.

BANQUET ROLLS

If you have contact with a Wholesaler either with a card or through a friend or business man, then paper banquet rolls can be obtained. These are long lengths of paper table cloth and are very easy to use and look very nice. If you are using disposable plates, then when it comes to clearing up, all you have to do is to remove anything for washing up and just bundle the rest together for disposal. But even where you are using china and glass, it is still easier to use banquet rolls – and cheaper!

SKIRTING THE TOP TABLE

Before you place the tablecloth over the tables, it looks much better if you lay a length of banquet roll along the front of the top table so that it touches the floor.

This looks much tidier, and the principal guests can kick their shoes off if they want to! It really does look much more professional. If you are doing this, then you will need scissors (for banquet roll) and Sellotape to fix the 'skirt' to the table. The guests' tables do not have this skirt, unless there are guests only sitting on one side of the table.

Table Plan

A table plan is most important at any wedding, whether it is a formal wedding breakfast or a buffet. It tells guests where they should sit and you can use it to introduce each side of the family to one another, or to keep arguing factions apart.

The Bride and Groom must sit in the middle of the top table and therefore, you must have an even number of people on the top table. If there is an odd number, say nine (i.e. Bride, Groom, Best Man, two mothers, two fathers and two Bridesmaids) then one extra person can be asked to sit on the top table. Eight people across the top table does not give enough width for two sprigs (tables coming away from the top table). However, if there are eleven or thirteen, then one person can sit round the corner – probably a young Bridesmaid who needs to be near her parents, who can then sit on the sprig, but next to their daughter.

TOP TABLE

Groom's Mother	Bride's Father	Best Man	Bride	Groom	Chief Bridesmaid	Groom's Father	Bride's Mother

The closest family sit nearest to the top table, starting with grandparents (unless there is some need for them to be near the door or the toilet, due to age or infirmity – their preference should then be sought), then brothers, sisters, spouses and children then aunts, uncles and cousins, then friends.

Variations where parents are divorced have already been explained under an earlier chapter.

Be careful to draw your table plan out carefully and pin or stick it up somewhere in the hall, where the guests will see it after shaking hands with the receiving line, but not so close that it will cause 'bunching' at the end of the Line, whilst guests find their places.

LAYING THE TABLE

Normally at most halls the caretaker will get the tables and chairs out in the morning before you arrive. If not, the first job to do is to pull the tables into shape and to put the chairs round, so that the numbers fit the table (keep your rough copy of the table plan to work from, rather than ruin the one which is to be pinned up). Then skirt the top table and then cover the tops of the tables.

. Now add your decorations – ribbon hanging in loops at the front of the table and any flowers for the table centres.

Next take your place cards and put these in everyone's place. Then one person takes the knives, another the forks and sets the correct number of places. In the meantime someone should be in the kitchen making up the salads. As these are made up and cling-wrapped they are brought out and put in each place. This goes on until the tables are all laid. This should not take more than an hour. Now help can be given in the kitchen to get the rest of the salads out and to lay out the cups, starters, desserts, whatever is to be left in the kitchen (this should be kept to a minimum as most hall kitchens are small). If you are putting desserts and starters on the table, or mayonnaise in bowls, these should be cling-wrapped.

A young person can be put in charge of the clingwrapping.

What to do if anything goes wrong

SOMEONE FAILS TO DELIVER

Basically you must make sure that you have checked up on anyone who has been asked to deliver food, drink or equipment for the wedding – one month before, one week before and the final checks should be made on the day before. Allow extra time in case there are delays when specifying delivery times. However, if the meat does not turn up, send someone up to the local Supermarket, or ring them in advance asking for, say one hundred slices of cooked turkey and one hundred slices of ham, telling them that someone is leaving to collect it immediately. This should get instant re-action. If you have already paid in advance for the cold meat or whatever has not turned up, you should still have your contingency fund to cover this extra expense.

Immediately anything is five minutes later than you had anticipated, telephone the supplier. Never let time slip by hoping it will turn up eventually.

Non-perishable items should have been delivered with plenty of time to spare. If the wholesaler does not have everything you require in stock you may have to wait for fresh supplies to arrive, but do ask again early in the last week.

Do not forget if you are in trouble never be afraid to ask for help. Always explain to people that it is for a wedding and you will find that they spring into action. If all else fails, ring a local caterer, they will tell you what to do.

If you have bought your meat the day before from a local supplier and you do not think it is fresh, ring him immediately and tell him. If you have told him that you require your meat for the following day, he should have taken responsibility to make sure that it will stay fresh, provided you have kept it refrigerated. If you have stored it in the freezer, you could be in a difficult position. If in doubt, and it is still during the week, ring the Local Public Health Inspector, or Environmental Health Inspector. If nothing can be done immediately, replace the meat, from your contingency fund.

DROOPY LETTUCE

Droopy lettuce can sometimes be revived with just a few ice cubes in the water. If not, then it must be replaced. If you feel you have been cheated you should complain to the supplier and try to get him to replace it, but if not, do not waste time, just replace it out of your contingency fund and argue about it later. The Trading Standards Officer may also help you after the event.

INSUFFICIENT QUANTITIES

Everyone seems to worry about not ordering enough food in advance. If you are making up your salads, you will be able to ensure that there is enough to go round. If you find you need a few more tomatoes or some slices of ham, you can always run up the road to the shops and buy some. Even on Sundays there are usually a few corner shops open who stock most of these sorts of things. If this is not possible, then reduce other guests' plates to make up the extra.

Catering

UNEXPECTED GUESTS

We often find that guests who have said they cannot come and even some who were not invited will suddenly turn up at a wedding. This is really most embarrassing and ill mannered of the guests. The only thing to do is to tell them the truth. 'We were under the impression that you were not coming and we have not therefore made provision for you in the catering and although we are happy for you to stay, we regret that we are unable to provide you with a meal.' Remember they are in the wrong by turning up unexpectedly. It is possible that some guests will have failed to arrive anyway, in which case, these unexpected guests can take their places. Unexpected guests most usually turn up when it is known that the reception is to be a buffet. It is best, therefore, to let everyone know that there is to be a table plan, so that if you have to ring round to guests who have not replied definitely one way or the other, you can explain that you are ringing round to get final names and numbers for the tableplan. The Groom's mother should say the same thing, whether you are having a table plan or not. You can always say that you changed your mind at the last minute, if anyone is rude enough to enquire as to why there was not a table plan after all.

NON-ARRIVAL OF GUESTS

No hold-ups should be allowed because guests have not arrived. It is their responsibility to get to the church and from the church to the reception. Maps can be given to assist and the Best Man and Ushers can make arrangements for guests who know the way from the church to the reception to travel with those who do not. They are also responsible for making sure that everyone has a lift from the church. If there are insufficient vehicles, then the Best Man orders taxis. This can be done in advance, or a telephone box located, together with the local cab firm number in case the need arises.

However, if anyone does not turn up, the Bride should not wait outside the church, nor should the commencement of the wedding breakfast be unduly delayed. The reason for this is an unhappy one. If anything tragic has occurred this detail is kept from the Bride for as long as possible and an undue wait for the commencement of the wedding reception draws attention to a guest's absence.

If anyone has a car accident or is taken seriously ill, the Bride should only be told the minimum, to keep her happy, as should the two mothers and the two fathers (if possible). That is to say, if anyone has died, the Bride should be told that they are only slightly ill, or slightly injured, so that she can enjoy the rest of her wedding day. After all, if anyone has most regrettably died, there is nothing that can be done about it and it would not have been their wish that their demise should ruin a wedding day. We only mention this point as on one occassion, something of this nature did occur and the above arrangements were made. The Bride was told that the person concerned was ill and when she returned from honeymoon she was told that he had died during her honeymoon. Brides can get very upset about people dying on their wedding day, when emotions are very near the surface, so care should be taken with these situations. In this instance the man who had died was not close to the Bride, but knowing he had actually died at her wedding would have wrecked her wedding day and her honeymoon.

CATERING

Caterer 1   **Menu**   Price per head £

Name   No. of Guests

Address   **Total £**

Tel   VAT

Contact

Caterer 2   **Menu**   Price per head £

Name   No. of Guests

Address   **Total £**

Tel   VAT

Contact

Caterer 3   **Menu**   Price per head £

Name   No. of Guests

Address   **Total £**

Tel   VAT

Contact

Caterer chosen

Name

Address

Tel

Menu agreed

Price per head

Total Cost

VAT

Total   £

Less Deposit   £

Balance due   £

on _____ (date)

DOING THE CATERING MYSELF			
Item	Quantity	Price per g/lb/each	Total
Lettuce			
Cucumber			
Onions			
Coleslaw cabbages			
Carrots			
Rice			
Stir and Fry			
Meat Turkey			
Ham			
Beef			
Other			
Trifles			
Whole chickens			
Flans			
Gateaux			
Prawns			
Beetroot			
Grapefruit			
Eggs			
After Dinner Mints			
Coffee			
Milk/cream/coffee creamer			
Sugar			
Cream for desserts			
Wine			
Sherry			
Champagne			
Whisky			
Vodka			
Gin			
Brandy			
Bacardi			
Dark Rum			
Pernod			
Lager			
Bitter			
Light Ale			
Brown Ale			

DOING THE CATERING MYSELF			
Item	Quantity	Price per g/lb/each	Total
Guinness			
American Ginger			
Lemonade			
Cola			
Tonic			
Soda			
Cordials Lime			
Peppermint			
Orange			
Blackcurrant			
Lemon			
Fresh fruit juice			
Orange			
Grapefruit			
Pineapple			
Tomato			
Bread			
Rolls			
Butter			
Cheese			
Sausage rolls			
Savoury flans (Quiches)			
Veal and ham (Gala) Pies			
Crisps			
Nuts			
Pickled Onions			
Sweet pickles			
Mustard pickles			
Gherkins			
Biscuits/cakes			
Disposables			
Dinner Plates			
Side Plates			
Bowls			
Cups			
Trifle cups			
Knives			
Forks			

DOING THE CATERING MYSELF			
Item	Quantity	Price per g/lb/each	Total
Dessert Spoons			
Tea Spoons			
Hireages			
Dinner Plates			
Dessert Plates			
Side Plates			
Cups and saucers			
Sundae dishes			
Wine glasses			
Sherry glasses			
Beer glasses			
Champagne glasses			
Knives and forks			
Butter Knives			
Dessert Spoons and Forks			
Tea spoons			
Coffee spoons			
Salad Bowls			
Trifle Bowls			
Flats (large plates for meat, sandwiches, etc.)			
Coffee jugs			
Tea pots			
Cream jugs			
Milk jugs			
Hot water jugs			
Sugar bowls			
Ash trays			
Salt and pepper sets			
Candelabra			
Cake stand and knife			
Tea Urn/Baby Burco			
Optics			
Staff			
Waitresses			
Major Domo			
Bar Staff			

Transport

Transport to the church, from the church to the reception and from the reception to the honeymoon hotel is quite important. Not only do the Bride and Groom have to be organised to arrive in the correct sequence with the Bridesmaids, but there are also a large number of people to move about. As already suggested, those with cars should be given maps to show them where the church is and where the reception is to be held. Those coming by public transport can be provided with bus and train timetables, together with maps of stations, taxi ranks and bus stops, bearing in mind that it is their responsibility to get themselves to the church.

From the point of view of practicality any car will do to convey the Bride to the church. However, many Brides prefer to choose some mode of transport, which only their wedding day will give them the opportunity of travelling in.

HIRING

If you are hiring a vehicle to take you to church, then you should be hiring from a bona fide hire company. You should check that they are registered in accordance with local bye-laws and are insured for hire and reward. The only possible exception to this is where the photographer provides a Rolls Royce as a free offer with the photography.

Horse and Carriage

FOR

From a photographer's point of view, there is nothing so quaint and pretty as the Bride arriving at church in a carriage. Many Brides like to take this opportunity of riding in a carriage for the sake of being different and for the very effect it gives, especially if the Bride is wearing an Edwardian, or a Victorian outfit.

AGAINST

A horse and carriage is much more expensive to hire than any other mode of transport. If you are a long way from a stables, it is unlikely that the horses will be able to pull the carriage for many miles and they would therefore transport the horses in a horsebox and the carriage on a lorry, which can make it even more expensive. If the church is a long way from the Bride's house, then her ride to church in a horse drawn carriage could take a very long time. The photographer may also charge more as he will have to start work earlier and probably will have to wait a long time at the church for the Bride to arrive. This would also mean that if the Bridesmaids were travelling by car that it would be difficult to judge the time for them to set off by car.

The same thing obviously follows if the reception is a long way from the church, because guests today do not wait to make sure that the Bride arrives first at the Reception. Whenever the Bride travels by carriage, guests are likely to overtake her by car, although they should follow. If this occurs, then arrangements should be made for the guests to have their sherry in another room, so that the Bride has time to arrive and compose herself, together with the other principal guests in a receiving line in the actual room where the Wedding Breakfast is to be held.

Another thing to bear in mind is that carriages, unlike cars, do not have heating in them and a carriage and pair should not be considered, except when the weather is likely to be at its warmest and dryest. Most carriages do have hoods if the weather is wet, but the main effect is lost if the hood has to be put up.

ROLLS ROYCES

The Rolls Royce is still the most popular choice for a Bride to travel to her wedding in, affording both comfort and style. However, care should be taken in hiring certain models of Rolls Royces. The older Silver Cloud has a great deal of room at the back for a Bride who has a hooped petticoat and a long veil, some of the more recent models are not so accommodating. You should always go to see the vehicle you are hiring well in advance of booking and again just before the wedding. Firstly to see how much room there is in the back for your dress (you do not want to arrive at the church all crumpled up) and to see that the vehicle is in good condition. The rate charged is no measurement of this. The second visit is to make sure that no damage or deterioration has occurred to the vehicle.

Vintage cars, particularly Rolls Royces, are a reasonable compromise between the new and the old, being both picturesque and warm and comfortable. It is not usually much more expensive to hire a Vintage Rolls than it is to hire a new one, but these are very popular and get booked up well in advance.

Other Cars

The Mercedes is a very popular car and so is the Jaguar, but both of these afford less room in the back for the Bride and her accoutrements. However, these are not a lot cheaper than the Rolls Royce and thought could be given to asking the Rolls Royce to make two trips – one for the Bridesmaids and one for the Bride to the church (other arrangements would have to be made for the Bridesmaids to go to the Reception, perhaps with the Bride's father) or for a friend with a new car to take the Bridesmaids, so that the Bride uses the Rolls Royce.

COLOURS OF CARS

Although white is the most popular colour for a bridal car, these days, other colours are becoming popular. The ideal colour is black as this draws attention to the white of the Bride by contrasting with her, whereas with white, the two whites together can make one white look creamy, whilst the other looks blue. You could try telephoning around to see if anyone hires out, say, a blue car if your Bridesmaids are wearing blue.

How Many Cars and Who Goes By Car

Ideally everyone goes by car to the church in the principal wedding party. The Bride goes with her father. The Bride's mother with the Bridesmaids. The Groom and the Best Man travel together, and the Groom's parents. If you wish to cut down on expenses it is perfectly all right for the Groom and the Best Man, and the Groom's parents to travel in their own cars or for them to use taxis. Taxis can also be hired for the Bride and her father and the Bride's mother and the Bridesmaids. This is unusual as other guests with cars are usually pressed into service to take the Bride and her father and the Bride's mother and Bridesmaids. The Groom usually has a friend with a car who can pick him and the Best Man up and some of the Groom's family can usually take his parents with them.

If you do not have a car, but the Groom or Bride do drive, then a car can be hired for the day, or for a longer duration, if the Bride and Groom need a car for their honeymoon. Self-drive hire can usually be found under that title in the Yellow Pages, or many of the main dealers hire out cars as well. This can work out quite economically as the Groom's parents can travel from home with him in this hire car, and the Best Man can then take over and drive them to the reception.

A check should be made if a lot of guests are coming to the church to ensure that there will be enough places in cars for everyone to travel. If possible guests with cars should be contacted and asked if they will take 'Aunty Ethel' from the church to the reception before the wedding, if possible. If not, it is up to the Best Man and Ushers to sort this out, whilst the photographs are being taken, bearing in mind that the Best Man will be expected to be in quite a few of these photographs. This is another reason why it is important to have an Usher from each side of the family, so that they will recognise those with cars and those without.

Timing

We are assuming that the wedding is at 3 p.m. and the journey to the church will take five minutes. This is about the normal length of time as parishes today are quite small. We are assuming that guests are being taken by other guests, and that the Bride and Groom and relatives are being taken to the church by friends. If you are hiring a car, leave the timing up to them. They will know when you should be leaving. If the journey is longer, then allowance should be made for this. If you are in any doubt, make a trial run on the Saturday before your wedding at the same time as you will be getting married to check exactly how much time you need. Do not forget to check for any processions, carnivals, etc. (the curse of the town centre on a summer Saturday).

The Bridesmaids with the Bride's mother leave at 2.40 p.m. If there are more than three Bridesmaids, two cars will be needed, the Bride's mother travelling with the youngest Bridesmaids.

The Bride with her father should leave no later than 2.50, even if the journey takes only five minutes. When the Bride arrives at the church, the photographer will want to take a photograph of her getting out of the car, possibly one going up the church path and the 'processional shot' of her and her father, with the Vicar at the church door and the Bridesmaids lined up behind. If you do not get to church five minutes early, then the photographer will not have time to take these photographs, because weddings usually start on time as there may be more weddings to follow, which will also need to start without delay.

The Groom and Best Man should arrange to arrive at the church, slightly before the Bridesmaids at about 2.40, leaving home at about 2.30. It is better that they and the Ushers should be there too early, rather than too late. As the Ushers and Best Man have to look after the guests, it is essential that they are there before they start to arrive. This will also enable the photographer to photograph the Groom and Best Man together and then with the Ushers, so that the Groom and Best Man can proceed into Church to see the Vicar in the vestry, leaving the photographer to photograph the arrival of the Bridesmaids.

Other guests at the wedding should arrive between 2.40 and 2.50 and not stand around outside the Church talking. It is up to the Ushers to hand them their buttonhole and hymn book/Order of Service and direct them to their seats, taking them in and showing them where to sit. The Groom's family sit on the right side of the church (your right as you face the altar) the Bride's family to the left. The Bride's brothers and sisters (if any) sit in the front pew leaving nearest the aisle for their mother and father; the Bride's father joins the Bride's mother after he has given the Bride away. This only varies if the Bridesmaids are going to sit down, in which case the Bride's family (brothers and sisters) sit in the second pew, and only her mother sits in the front pew. The Groom and Best Man sit in the front pew and his family all sit in the second pew with his parents sitting in the two seats closest to the aisle. The closer the family, the nearer they sit to the front. Friends should be shown to pews further back. The ushers should have an idea of how many members of their particular family are expected at the church. The Vicar will know how many people sit in a pew, and it can then be worked out how many pews will be needed for the family. The Ushers then take care to ensure that all the pews are filled. If possible, people with small children should be seated near to side aisles, if there are no side aisles, the centre aisle, so that if the children start to cry, they can be taken outside easily.

In this way, by being led in by the Ushers, most of the guests will go into the church and sit down. Anyone who refuses on the grounds that they want to take photographs should be told firmly that the Bride or her mother 'does not wish anyone to see the Bride until she comes into Church''. If anyone is still rude enough to refuse to go in they should be told, '——— will be very upset and I am sure you would not want to upset her on his/her daughter's wedding day'.

Transport

Going to the Reception

BRIDE AND GROOM

The Bride and Groom leave first in the car in which the Bride came to church with her father.

THE BRIDESMAIDS

The Bridesmaids travel in the car in which they came to church. They follow the Bride and Groom.

BRIDE'S PARENTS

The Bride's parents are always a problem. The Bride's mother travels with the Bridesmaids again. The Bride's father can join her if there is room in the car. If not, if the Groom's parents came in their own car, then the Bride's parents can leave with them. However, sometimes the father of the Bride likes to drive his own car from the church and this means that in the morning someone has to follow him in his car to the church and bring him home, leaving his car at the church.

If the Best Man is driving the Groom's car or his own car, as an alternative the Bride's father can travel with him.

The Bride's father and Best Man follow the Bridesmaids.

THE GROOM'S PARENTS

The Groom's Parents leave by the same means as they arrived and follow the Bride's parents.

OTHER GUESTS

The Ushers then sort everyone into their respective cars, including anyone who does not have transport, delaying the guests as tactfully as possible to enable the Bride and Groom to get away and to have their photographs taken with the cake and so that the receiving line can then be formed and the guests all greeted one by one by each member of the Bridal Party. If there are young Bridesmaids it is not necessary to include them in the receiving line, unless they want to stay. The Chief Bridesmaid is all that is necessary, and perhaps grown up Bridesmaids.

Leaving for the Honeymoon

BY TAXI

It is best to arrange well in advance for a taxi to collect the Bride and Groom from the Reception to take them on honeymoon and do point out to the taxi company what the taxi is for (some will put 'Just Married' on the back of the taxi, which is a nice touch – if necessary the Best Man can ring the taxi rank and ask for this to be done, if he can find which taxi rank has been employed, although, strictly speaking it is his job to arrange for transport from the Reception).

BY A FRIEND'S CAR

If a friend, or the Best Man is to take the Bride and Groom to the station, airport or hotel, then they should make sure that they are well aware of how to get there. There is nothing worse than getting lost on your way on honeymoon, especially when you are both longing to be alone, and maps have to be got out, or you have to stop and ask someone where a certain hotel is. Anyone taking on this duty should be careful not to drink – an accident would be disastrous, let alone being breathalysed and then arrested, leaving the Bride and Groom stranded.

When the Bride and Groom reach their destination, the 'chauffeur' should then depart and no matter how entreated by the Bride and Groom to stay for a drink, he should politely excuse himself.

BY OWN CAR

Many Grooms ruin the fun of a wedding, by hiding their own car so that it cannot be decorated, but this is not necessary if care is taken by the Best Man to ensure that nothing is put on the car which will damage the paintwork (see next page).

Again, the Groom should be quite sure that he knows where he is going and that he has not had too much to drink. Basically he should drink only soft drinks for four hours before he is going to drive.

Decoration of the Honeymoon Car

Decorating the car is a tradition, which if done right can be very amusing for the Bride and Groom and guests alike. When a car can be identified as being driven by 'Just Marrieds', then other drivers have the opportunity of joining in the celebrations and will wave and hoot. This can be a very happy experience. However, care needs to be taken that no damage will occur to the car, or passengers, or any other road users.

Never use lipstick on a car, nor on the glass as it stains, especially on white cars. Under no circumstances should anything be written on the paintwork of a car. Notices can be written and tied on with string. The artificial snow, which is used at Christmas for decorating windows, can be used for writing on car windows, but care should be taken to ensure that this is not used to such an extent as to obscure the driver's vision.

Crepe paper, toilet paper and confetti can be used to decorate the car, although beware of dyes running from these in wet weather as these can stain the paintwork. Care should also be taken to ensure that when this paper breaks it will not fly up onto the windscreen, obscuring the driver's view. Balloons are alright, but these should be on long, loosely tied string, so that they can float off. Shoes (old ones) are better than using tin cans for decoration, tied loosely, so that they will fall off the car before it leaves the car park. If this does not happen and on leaving the car park, the shoes are still attached to the bumper (the best place to attach these, so that they can easily be removed), then the driver should stop and remove them, having given the guests the pleasure of decorating the car and seeing the Bride and Groom drive off (the Best Man should ensure that the driver, probably the Groom, has a pair of scissors to facilitate this).

Never put stones in the hub caps. This is extremely dangerous. We have known the hub cap to come off and a stone to fly out and smash someone else's windscreen – it could have hit a child's head! This is just too dangerous.

CAR/CARRIAGE HIRE

Hirer 1

Name _____ Make of Car _____ Colour _____
Address _____ Second Car _____ Colour _____
Tel _____ Cost of main car £
Cost of second car £
Extras £
VAT £

Hirer 2

Name _____
Address _____ Make of Car _____ Colour _____
Tel _____ Second Car _____ Colour _____
Cost of main car £
Cost of second car £
Extras £
VAT £

Hirer 3

Name _____ Make of Car _____ Colour _____
Address _____ Second Car _____ Colour _____
Tel _____ Cost of main car £
Cost of second car £
Extras £
VAT £

Car decided on
Name and Address _____

Total Cost £
VAT £
Deposit paid £
Balance due on _____ (date) £

The Big Day

THE MORNING

For this section we will assume that the wedding is to take place in a local Church at 3.00 p.m., with the reception reasonably close by and that the Bride and her family are organising the reception themselves, with a couple of members of staff to help, and that they have chosen to use the type of 'sit-down' buffet we have suggested under 'Catering'. Obviously, if caterers are employed then they should be instructed carefully about how you want things done to ensure that they know when and where everything should take place.

8.00 a.m.   Bride rises and has breakfast. This is important, no matter how little you feel like eating breakfast, you should eat. You will be offered drinks all day and an empty stomach can lead to frayed nerves later on and even fainting, neither of which are desirable on a wedding day. Then the Bride should bath.

215

9.00 a.m.	Hairdressers for the Bride and her mother and any sisters who are Bridesmaids. Collect your flowers if they are not to be delivered.
10.30 a.m.	Bride and her mother meet Bride's father at the hall. Start to lay tables, make up salads.
12.00	Bride and mother leave for home – anyone else can stay, except Bridesmaids.
12.15 p.m.	Bride and mother arrive home. Lunch and cup of tea – sandwich and cake will do – plenty of carbohydrate for energy. Sandwiches can have been made up the day before and cling wrapped and put in the fridge.
12.30 p.m.	Bride and mother to apply make-up. If you have to varnish your nails, do this whilst your mother is getting the lunch and then eat your lunch carefully, then put on your make-up.
1.15 p.m.	Bride's father arrives home. (If he has stayed at hall to complete laying out of catering and to await arrival of staff at 1.00 p.m. to continue with preparations.) Bride and her mother arrange her headdress and veil.
1.30 p.m.	Bride gets into dress, helped by mother and Bridesmaids. Arrival of other Bridesmaids, fully dressed. Bride's mother must get dressed now!
1.45 p.m.	Arrival of photographer. Bride's father must be getting dressed by now. The bathroom and bedroom will both be clear as the Bride's mother is already dressed.
2.30 p.m.	Bride has photograph taken at the door with her father and photographer departs.
2.35 p.m.	Arrival of Ushers at church.

2.40 p.m.	Arrival of Groom and Best Man at church. Photographer arrives at church. Photographs of Groom and Best Man, who immediately go into church. Bridesmaids leave the Bride's house, with Bride's mother. Guests start arriving.
2.45 p.m.	Arrival of Bride's mother and Bridesmaids. Photographs.
2.50 p.m.	All guests should have arrived at Church by now, and have been shown to their seats. Mother of Bride accompanied to seat by Usher, who returns to position at church door. Bride and father leave home.
2.55 p.m.	Arrival of Bride and father at church. Photographs.
3.00 p.m.	Bride and father enter church, followed by Bridesmaids.

THE CEREMONY

This is the reason why everyone is there. It does not matter if you are not wearing a white dress or carrying flowers, if there are Bridesmaids or not, whether there is to be a reception and honeymoon, or if you are going straight home after the ceremony. The most important part of the whole day is that you and your groom, in the presence of two witnesses over the age of eighteen, stand before a priest and say your vows. Although the rest of the day may be light and frivolous, without the ceremony there would be no reason for it. The ceremony is very serious and should be treated as such. You are making very solemn vows about the way you intend to spend the rest of your life.

Line-up for Procession into Church

Church Door
Vicar
Bride's father, Bride
Page
Small Bridesmaids
Adult Bridesmaids
Chief Bridesmaid

Whether the Vicar comes to the church door or not, immediately the organist strikes up the first chord of the wedding music the Bride and her father set off up the aisle, and the congregation all stand up, and the Groom and Best man move slightly forward and out into the aisle to join the Bride and her father.

The rest of the Congregation stand as well. The Groom may turn to look at his Bride as she advances up the aisle. When the Bride reaches the steps of the Altar where the Vicar is standing, the Chief Bridesmaid comes forward to take the Bride's bouquet. This is usually a good time to remove the veil from the Bride's face and the Chief Bridesmaid can help her if she first hands her own posy to one of the other Bridesmaids. Having removed the veil from the Bride's face, she then takes the Bride's bouquet and returns to her place at the back of the Bridesmaids. It may be a good idea to ask the Vicar if there is any particular time when he prefers the veil to be pulled back. The Groom himself can remove the veil if the Vicar allows a moment in the service for the Groom to kiss the Bride, in which case the Groom removes the veil from the Bride's face, before kissing her. However, the kissing part of the ceremony is very rarely performed these days. If the Vicar does allow this, the kiss should be light and affectionate and not long and passionate, which might be embarrassing.

If there are any very young Bridesmaids who are going to want to sit down or stand with their parents, then it is sometimes better if they follow the Chief Bridesmaid, so that their parents can sit in the middle of the Church and scoop them up if they start to get fractious.

The Congregation remain standing and the Priest begins by addressing the Congregation, who he will then invite to sit. There is then an explanation of how the church regards marriage. There is a part in this section which refers to children, but if you are past childbearing age or cannot have children for any reason, then you can ask for this part to be left out.

The next part is most important, when the Priest will ask everyone in the congregation if they know of any legal reason why the Bride and Groom should not be married. It is imperative that everyone remains silent, because if the Priest hears anything which might sound like an objection to the marriage, then he must stop the ceremony and investigate.

The Vicar will then ask the Bride and Groom whether they know of any reason' why they should not marry and provided both answer 'No', then this is the last hurdle overcome and the marriage may then proceed.

The Bride and Groom then make their vows, repeating each section after the Priest. This part is known as 'The Marriage'. If you are in any doubt about the words you have to say, you can ask the Priest a week or two before the wedding if you can borrow a copy of the marriage vows. However, you should not try to learn your vows off by heart, but use the opportunity of looking at the words to ensure that you do mean what you will have to say. Do not be frightened of 'fluffing' your lines. Both Prince Charles and Princess Diana did this and yet both appear to be very happily married and no one thought any the less of them.

There are a number of different versions of the marriage service, so if you have a preference, do not be afraid to ask your Vicar if he would be kind enough to use the one that you prefer.

Next comes the 'giving away' ceremony. This does not have to be done. If you do not have a father, then your mother can give you away, it does not have to be a man, or alternatively you may go to the altar unaccompanied.

You should give a great deal of thought as to whether you want to promise to 'obey'. Very few Brides promise to obey their husbands today because these vows are very solemn and binding and to promise to 'obey' when you have no intention of doing so is a hypocrisy, which at such a solemn moment would appear to be inappropriate.

The Vicar will then bless the ring or rings, and the Bride and Groom exchange rings, still repeating the words the Vicar is saying.

The Priest will then announce to the Congregation that you

are now husband and wife and will give you a short blessing. When the priest says 'Amen', so does the rest of the Congregation.

It is possible that at this point the Registers may be signed, thus completing all the legal formalities, but some Priests feel that this breaks up the Service and therefore prefer to do this at the end.

Now comes the Blessing and the Bride and Groom proceed to the Altar with the Priest and everyone else kneels (except the Bridesmaids if there is no pew for them to move into). It is permissible for anyone who finds it difficult or painful to kneel to remain seated in their pew and to bow their head. Various prayers are said for the future happiness of the Bride and Groom. At the very end the Lord's Prayer is said.

If the register was not signed in the middle of the service, then the Bride and Groom, together with both sets of parents, the Best Man and the Bridesmaids go into the vestry to sign the register. In more and more churches today, the register is being signed in front of the congregation. Do not forget to have an idea of who you are going to ask to be witnesses, say the two mothers, the two fathers, or the Best Man and Chief Bridesmaid and to have warned them in advance. This saves a lot of discussion, and avoids insulting anyone.

The bridal party then 'recess' down the aisle in this order:

		Altar		
Groom's Father				Groom's Mother
Bride's Father				Bride's Mother
		Smallest Bridesmaids		
Best Man				Chief Bridesmaid
		Groom	Bride	

It is also correct for the Groom's father to escort the Bride's mother and the Bride's father to escort the Groom's mother.

The Best Man and Chief Bridesmaid should walk very slowly behind the Bride and Groom, giving them a good 'head start'.

220

If the photographer stops the Bride and Groom for a photograph, then the Best Man and Bridesmaids stop. If the photographer is trying to take photographs in the church doorway, the Best Man just holds everyone up until the photographer is ready to let all the guests through the door. The Ushers should have moved outside the church to clear the doorway of anyone 'hanging about' outside. The Ushers then direct the guests to a position where they will not be directly in the line of sight of the Bride and Groom, whilst the photographs are being taken. Enquiries can be made of the photographer before the ceremony as to where he would like the guests to stand.

Photographers usually spend twenty minutes or more taking the wedding pictures outside the church. The ceremony should have taken between twenty and thirty minutes.

Church Music
It is no longer necessary to have the Wedding March and the Bridal March. Alternatives may be used – Crown Imperial, the Prince of Denmark's March, Pomp and Circumstance March – all are popular alternatives. Discuss your ideas with the Organist.

Leaving the Church
First the Bride and Groom leave, then the Bridesmaids (unless the car taking the Bride and Groom has to return to collect the Bridesmaids – this is not a good idea) with the Bride's mother, or both parents, then the Best Man, with Bride's father, if he is not travelling with the Bridesmaids. Then the Groom's parents. *Nobody* else leaves until the bridal party have left, no matter what excuse! – except the photographer.

THE WEDDING BREAKFAST

The Bride and Groom should arrive at the reception between 4.15 p.m. and 4.30 p.m. if the wedding took place at 3.00 p.m.

First the photographer will want the photographs of the Bride and Groom with the cake, so that he can get away, and the reception can progress.

Receiving Line

The order in which people stand for the receiving line is this:

Door
Bride's mother
Groom's father
Bride
Groom
Groom's mother
Bride's father
Chief Bridesmaid
Best Man
Usher
Bridesmaid

In this way the Bride's mother greets a member of her family and introdces them to the Groom's father. If the guest is a member of the Groom's family, then the Groom's father introduces them to the Bride's mother. The receiving line is arranged so that there is a man standing next to a woman and a member of each side of the family, alternating all the way down the line, so that everyone gets introduced.

If something not quite so formal is required, then the Bride's mother (as hostess) stands at the door with the Bride and Groom. The Groom then introduces all members of his family to both the Bride and her mother.

Introductions are made, as follows, with appropriate alterations. This is the Bride's mother greeting her sister and introducing her to the Groom's father. 'Hello, Lizzie. May I introduce my son-in-law's father, George Smith. George – my sister, Elizabeth Jones.'

The Bride will follow the same procedure, introducing her aunt to her husband: 'Hello, Aunt Lizzie. May I introduce my husband David Brown. David – my mother's sister, Elizabeth Jones.'

Background Music

If you are providing background music, either played from a

tape cassette, or by the disco, this should be kept light and romantic. Do not try to turn the music up during the introductions so that it can be heard above the talking, or else no one will be able to hear themselves speak.

Receiving Presents

As guests arrive they will be bringing presents with them. Wedding gifts should be given before the wedding, but today, many guests bring their gifts with them, so a table near the Bride to take the presents is a good idea. When given a present just say 'Thank you so much, it looks very interesting. I shall look forward to opening it.'

Serving the Sherry

The sherry should be strategically placed at the end of the Receiving Line, so that each guest is given a glass either by a waitress or the Best Man or Chief Bridesmaid.

Entry of the Bride and Groom

When the introductions are over and all the guests are drinking their sherry and looking for their seats – on the table plan and then finding their place at the table, this is the Bride and Groom's opportunity to quietly disappear into another room, into the kitchen (if you must) up on to the stage (if there is one), anywhere where the guests cannot see them – even outside, if necessary. Then the head waitress (if she feels confident enough) or the Bride's father, or the Best Man – the Groom's father can even be given this duty – knocks on the table three times and announces 'Ladies and Gentlemen will you please take your seats'. A few minutes needs to be given to allow them to settle down again.

Then whoever is doing the announcing knocks three times on the table again, standing at the doors, behind which the Bride and Groom are carefully concealed and announces: 'Ladies and Gentlemen, will you please stand to greet the Bride and Groom, Mr and Mrs David Brown.'

Grace

When the Bride and the Groom reach their seats they remain standing as do the rest of the 'Top Table'. The announcement is then made 'Ladies and Gentlemen will you please remain standing for Grace to be said by Mr (or Mrs) _____'. If you have a Vicar present, it is customary to ask him to say grace.

The best grace to use is short and simple:

'*For what we are about to receive may the Lord make us truly thankful.*'

Everyone says '*Amen*'.

Then the first two courses are served, if it is to be a three course meal. The next thing is:

Cutting the Cake

Between the main course and the dessert the Bride and Groom are asked to cut the cake. The Best Man will stand and say 'Ladies and Gentlemen, if I can have your attention for just one moment. It is my pleasant duty to announce that the Bride and Groom are now going to cut the cake.' The Best Man should stand to make this announcement. The reason the cake is cut at this time is that this gives the staff time, during the serving and consumption of the dessert, to cut up the wedding cake to serve with the coffee.

If it is not possible to cut the cake at this point, which it will not be with any form of buffet, then the cake is cut after the food has been consumed but before the speeches. If there is insufficient time to serve the cake at this stage it can be reserved until the evening buffet if there is to be one.

TO CUT THE CAKE

Both for the photographs and for the real cutting of the cake, there is an easy way to do this, so that Bride and Groom both press on the knife together without the Bride getting her hands squashed. It sounds complicated, but if in doubt have a practice on Mum's next Victoria sandwich.

The Bride puts her right hand on top of the handle of the knife. The Groom puts his right hand on top of the Bride's right hand (it is easiest to stand slightly to her right, but behind her). The Groom's left hand goes round the Bride's waist (this makes the whole thing look right). The Bride's left hand goes on top of the Groom's right (on her hand, on the knife).

Cigarettes and Smoking

CIGARETTES ON THE TABLE

To have cigarettes on the table, supplied by the hosts for the guests, was a very popular idea in the affluent sixties. However, today, not only are finances more restricted, but smoking is increasingly recognised as being an anti-social habit.

It is now not considered polite to provide cigarettes for your guests, although at the end of the meal it is customary to give your guests permission to smoke if they wish.

This announcement is usually made when the coffee is served.

NON-SMOKERS

If, for reason of ill health, it is important that no one smokes near to one of your guests, then you should make this clear to your guests. It may be possible to arrange the seating plan with a non-smoking area, thus keeping your smoking guests together. If it is important that no one smokes at all, make this plain in the form of an announcement, firmly but politely.

Speeches

BRIDE'S FATHER

1 Thanks everyone for coming to celebrate his daughter's marriage.
2 Welcomes Groom to the family.
3 Toasts the health and happiness of the Bride and Groom.
(The Bride's father speaks first. If there is no father her mother may do this, or whoever has given her away. Alternatively, if one uncle has given her away, another uncle can give the speech.

Ideally it should be someone who has known the Bride for most of her life. A brother could also do this.)

GROOM

1 Thanks the Bride's father for his good wishes.
2 Thanks everyone for coming and for their gifts.
3 Says thank you to both mothers for their help (whether they have or not) and if flowers are being presented, at this point he gives the flowers to the Bride's mother. The Bride hands the flowers to the Groom's mother.
4 Pays compliments to the Bridesmaids. Thanks the Best Man for helping him and the Chief Bridesmaid for helping the Bride.
5 Toasts the Bridesmaids.

BEST MAN

1 Thanks the Groom for his compliments on behalf of the Bridesmaids.
2 Reads telegrams (telemessages) and cards. (It is not a good idea to read all the cards – this can take hours and is extremely boring. If there are no telemessages, then only the cards from the parents, brothers and sisters and anyone who is absent from the wedding, either through illness, or because they live too far away, especially those living abroad.)
   When reading cards, it is important to read them all through first (All the wedding cards should be placed in front of the Best Man before the meal. Any which arrive well in advance of the wedding, can be given to him earlier), being careful to remove any whose words might offend anyone present at the wedding. If in doubt, play safe and do not read it.
3 One rather nice gesture I saw recently was, when the Best Man had finished his speech, for the whole of the Top Table to toast the guests, with the Best Man proposing the toast.
4 If, for happy reasons, someone is absent, then the Best Man can propose a toast to 'Absent friends'. However, if this is due to illness or bereavement, it is better not to do this.

The Big Day

It is permissible for other guests to make speeches if they wish to. Especially the Groom's father who may like to say how pleased he is that his son has married into the Bride's family (making absolutely no observations about any previous relationships he may have had) and to thank them for the lovely wedding.

Anyone else giving a speech should have this prepared and the Best Man should be warned, otherwise these things can go on and on and become boring. You always know when the guests are bored, because they start chatting noisily.

PREPARATION OF SPEECHES

It is imperative that speeches are prepared well in advance and each speech is checked by the Bride and Groom, to ensure that they are happy with what is being said. The Best Man's speech should be checked by the Bride's parents. It is easy for people to become offended by well-intentioned words. I remember an instance of this, where the Bride's father made an unprepared speech. The Groom's brother, being a caterer had given the Bride and Groom a wedding reception for one hundred guests as their wedding present. However, the Bride's father thanked 'My son-in-law's brother, his wife and the staff for all they have done at the reception', making it sound as if the Groom's brother and his wife had been hired as staff, instead of giving the very generous gift. This caused a huge rift in the family. So it is important that speeches are prepared and checked by anyone mentioned in them. Remember if in doubt, **leave it out**.

Each of the speeches should take up about three minutes. Anything shorter than three minutes sounds curt and disinterested anything longer tends to drag on. Three minutes does not sound very long, until you start to write your speech, then it seems like forever. However, never pad a speech out too much. If what you have to say comes to two and a half minutes, although it will sound a bit short, it is better than waffling.

Learn your speech off by heart. Take your speech with you, in case, under pressure, you forget your words and do not be embarrassed if you do. But if you learn your speech by heart this will enable you to keep your head up when you are speaking, thus avoiding mumbling.

Write your speech on postcards (the ones with lines on), one paragraph to each card and keep them in order. Number the cards (in case you drop them) in order. Then as you finish each paragraph you can just move that card to the bottom of the pile. If you do forget your words, you will only have a few lines to scan through to find your place.

The Wedding Presents

WHEN TO OPEN THEM

Many Brides leave the opening of their wedding presents until they are on their own with the Groom, after the wedding day. However, I always feel that this is unfair to the guests who have bought the presents. I always feel cheated if, when I have spent hours at the shops selecting a gift, I do not have the pleasure of watching the recipient open it.

Perhaps the best time to open the presents is after the speeches, when the hall is being cleared and prepared for the evening function, if there is to be one. This gives the guests something to do. With a 3.00 p.m. wedding, the hall will be being cleared at about 6.00 p.m. to 6.30 p.m., giving you between an hour and two hours before the evening guests arrive (a bit of a low point during the day), so I always think that this is the ideal time to open the presents.

MARKING THE PRESENTS

As the Bride and Groom open each present together, someone should stand nearby with Sellotape and a notepad and pencil (the Bride's mother, Chief Bridesmaid or Best Man). Where there are gift tags, these can be taped directly back onto the gift, unless this will damage it, or it may fall off. Not everyone uses gift tags, in which case the present and the name of the giver is entered into the notepad. You will need this information for your thank you letters and for later when your wedding guests come to visit your home.

MOVING THE PRESENTS
This is one job which is left up to someone else – the Best Man, Bride or Groom's father. It is a good idea to move these as soon as possible. There are two good reasons for this. The first is that it stops the presents from being damaged or mislaid and the second is not so obvious, but at most weddings the presents are numerous and heavy and by the end of the day, no one will have the energy to do the job. Also early in the evening, there will be plenty of people to lend a hand packing the presents into the car or cars.

CLEARING THE TABLES
If you are hiring the minimum amount of staff, or none at all, do not be afraid to get someone to announce that the tables are being cleared and could everyone lend a hand. It is true to say that 'many hands make light work' and quick work. If you need help in washing up – ask for volunteers – just make sure you have plenty of aprons, so that guests do not splash their clothes.

THE EVENING RECEPTION

The Bar
If it is at all possible the bar should be placed behind a hatch. In most halls there is a kitchen with a serving hatch. You may need to wait until the washing and clearing up is over before the bar can be set up, but this should take no longer than an hour, during which time the Bride can be opening her presents. The guests will just have had their wine to drink and their coffee, so they will not need refreshment. Many Brides and their parents feel that they must immediately open the bar as soon as the meal is over and this is not true. If necessary, a couple of bottles of wine can be left out with some glasses and a glass jug full of lemon or orange with glasses or paper cups, so that guests can

help themselves if they are thirsty. This can be left on the stage or on a table near to where the Bride is opening her presents (not so near that any might get spilled onto the presents).

However, if a kitchen hatch is not available tables can be used against a wall, with the tables surrounding the servers on three and a half sides (leaving space for the bar man to get in and out). The reason for this is to keep unauthorised guests from getting behind the bar and helping themselves and this causes chaos. Never place a bar anywhere near where people will be dancing. Not only do you stand a good chance of losing all or some of your drink, which can be expensive, but also guests could be injured.

STAFFING THE BAR

It really is better if you get staff in to cover the bar for you – perhaps those who have worked in the afternoon will stay on for the evening, or will know of someone who will do this. You need two people of mature age – one to serve and one to collect in glasses and wash up. Also if you have someone of responsible age, they will know when a guest has had enough to drink and can discreetly tell the Bride's father or Best Man.

A rota of guests is not a good idea, because as the evening goes on, guests forget that they are meant to be the next on duty, which usually means the Best Man, Groom or the fathers of the Bride and Groom end up doing the work.

No one from the bridal party should be serving behind the bar. Their most important job is to circulate and make sure the guests are enjoying themselves.

OPTICS

Much money and drink will be saved if you hire optics. This saves guests being given too much alcohol per drink, and also makes the drink last longer.

Entertainment

QUANTITY OF SOUND

If you are hiring a large hall, for a reception of one hundred
or more, then you need a disco with plenty of volume. Your
own stereo will not be heard. When booking a disco for a large
hall you should ask the D.J. how many watts per channel output
his equipment is capable of producing. This should be roughly
(very roughly) one watt per channel per guest at the reception.

MUSIC

If you are hiring a professional and experienced D.J., it is better
to leave the choice of music up to him. He will play a few records
and see which ones your guests respond well to, and then he will
play that sort of music. Obviously if there are certain records
which mean something special to you and your husband, you
can ask your D.J. to play those records. However, in the main,
leave the order and choice of music up to your D.J.

HIRING A BAND OR GROUP

If you wish to hire a band or group, the best people to contact
are the entertainment agencies. However, a band will want a
break. You cannot expect a band to play from 8.00 p.m. until
11.00 p.m. non-stop, so a disco or some alternative method of
playing music will be required. This can work out very expensive.

STARTING THE DANCING

It is important that the Bride and Groom start the dancing. You
should let your D.J. know that you want to do this and at what
time. If your guests are invited for 7.30 p.m., 8.00 p.m. would
appear to be the best time to start the dancing. Until that time
your D.J. will play background music (although this will be
livelier than that played during the meal). If you have a favourite
record which you and your husband like to dance to (it should
be a slow dance, so that you dance in one another's arms) you

should let the D.J. know that this is the record you wish to start the dancing to.

The D.J. will announce 'Ladies and Gentlemen, can I please have your attention. Your Bride and Groom, Mr and Mrs David Brown are about to start the dancing.' All the other guests then sit down. After the Bride and Groom have been dancing for a short while, the Bride's father asks the Groom's mother to dance and immediately the Groom's father asks the Bride's mother to dance (they should sit close together in order to facilitate this), then the Best Man and Chief Bridesmaid join in, then the brothers and sisters of the Bride and Groom (and their partners, one side asking the other to dance, if possible). The Ushers should join in, dancing with the other Bridesmaids, but if the guests are reluctant to dance it is up to them and the D.J. to get everyone else up.

The D.J. should be announcing all the time who should be joining the dancing next and then he says 'Now everyone else.' It is at this point if everyone remains seated that the Ushers start asking guests to dance.

Evening Buffet

When the hall is cleared, it is best to put the tables together which you will require for the evening buffet. These should be covered with banquet roll and the food (on cling wrapped plates) put on the table. Then cover this whole table and the food with another tablecloth (or banquet roll).

TIMING

If your photographer is to bring the photographs back in the evening, it is best to wait until he arrives to serve the evening buffet. The lights are then put on and a table found for him to lay out his photographs (if he is bringing them back, then guests will need the lights on to see the photographs, unless there is another room where the photographs can be laid out for viewing and guests to make their orders). Ask your D.J. to announce that the evening buffet is now served. At a 3.00 p.m. wedding, about 9.00 p.m. is about the right time to serve this, allowing for the time when the guests last ate, and for evening guests to arrive. The lights are still put on and the D.J. plays background music for about 20–30 minutes. If the photographer is still there you must wait until all your guests have seen the photographs and ordered, otherwise you can offend your guests who have not had this opportunity.

CUTTING THE CAKE

If you did not cut your wedding cake during the Wedding Breakfast, then you should ask the D.J. to announce (or let the Best Man announce) 'Ladies and Gentlemen, if I can have your attention for a very short while, the Bride and Groom are about to cut their wedding cake.' The cake is cut in the same way as described under 'Wedding Breakfast'. The cake should then be taken to the kitchen, and cut into portions wrapped in paper serviettes and put out on trays for the guests to help themselves. Alternatively, the Bride and Groom can distribute the cake themselves, from the trays, which gives them the chance to speak to each of the guests again.

Changing for the Evening/Honeymoon

HOTEL RECEPTIONS

Most hotels offer as part of the 'deal' a room for the Bride and Groom to change in. However, should they fail to make this offer, do not be afraid to ask if such a facility could be made available.

AT HOME

If you are getting changed at home when the reception is being held at home, it is customary for the Bride's mother to help her daughter to change, after which the Groom is allowed a few minutes alone with the Bride in her bedroom before they leave.

AT HALLS

In most local authority and public halls, there are few facilities for changing, so the Bride and Groom usually leave the reception for a short while in order to get changed. This amount of time should be limited to a minimum, as the celebrations tend to lose their impetus when the Bride and Groom are absent. The maximum amount of time you could be absent is about half an hour, including travelling time. If it is not possible to get home, get changed, and return to the Reception in that time, ask yourself whether you really need to go home to change. It is a good excuse to buy a new outfit (to go away in) – but why ruin your reception for that reason. Most Brides and Grooms spend the first night of their honeymoon in an hotel, whether they are going away on honeymoon, or spending their honeymoon at home. So why not arrive at the hotel in your wedding dress. Everybody loves a Bride! – and nobody will think the worse of you, at the hotel, for turning up in your wedding dress. If you feel you really could not stand to wear your wedding dress to the hotel, then why not take leave of your guests a little earlier and pop home to change on your way to the hotel.

However, if neither of these possibilities appeal to you and there is no separate room (or even the stage – sometimes there is a small room behind a stage) where you can change there is nothing for it, but to change in the loo! Get your mother to clear out the 'Ladies' first, so that you have plenty of space and privacy in which to change. Get a 'Temporarily Closed' notice made up (you can do this before the wedding if you know you are going to have to change in the loo – you can even write underneath in brackets 'Bride Changing'). And be quick. Remember guests will be drinking and their need for the space you are occupying may be urgent.

Do check out this aspect of the hall before you decide to buy a 'Going away' outfit, which you cannot use, without wasting a lot of your reception time.

Circulating

When meeting and mingling with your guests, your main aim should be to introduce guests to one another. When doing this you should try to mention something about them that the other person may be interested in. If a conversation strikes up between them, then pass onto another group, saying 'Will you excuse me I must go and speak to ＿＿ all I have said is "Hello" all day' or something like that. Do not just disappear. If a conversation does not begin, then say to one of your guests 'Excuse me but I must introduce ＿＿ (the other guest you have tried to introduce) to ＿＿'. In this way you should manage to get guests to mingle.

However, you should not feel that it is your duty to make sure that everyone is talking to everyone else. This is impossible. It is just nice to do this with guests who do not know anyone else at your wedding, like your friend from work, if she is the only one you have invited from work and does not know any of your other friends and family.

In a group of a hundred people if you spoke to each one for three minutes, it would take you five hours before you had spoken to them all.

The most important thing for the Bride and Groom to do is to keep dancing, either with each other, or your parents, or other guests. If someone is dancing, the rest will usually dance. If everyone is dancing, then nobody will be on their own. If, however, you have a single friend, or someone recently divorced, who is really lonely either the Bride or Groom (depending on the sex of the friend) can ask them to dance and quietly inform other members of the Bridal party (of the appropriate sex) that your friend is on his/her own, so that the other principal guests will ask him/her to dance.

Most important of all – make sure you dance with your new husband. All too often we see Brides and Grooms who see nothing of each other at the evening reception because they are so busy looking after their guests they forget themselves. Your wedding day really is the 'First Day of the Rest of Your Life' and you should be spending it together and sharing that experience, not serving behind the bar, ferrying guests to and from stations or cutting up the wedding cake. This is your wedding day – *enjoy it*. On this day only can you let everyone else help you. You can return their kindness at some other time. This will ensure that your wedding day is not only a success for you and your husband, but for the rest of the family and guests.

DON'T LET ANYTHING WORRY YOU

Many Brides spend half their wedding day worrying about what other people are doing. If a Bridesmaid does not turn up, or a guest, or someone is a bit off-hand in something they say, just ignore it. It really is as easy as that. There are very few things that can go wrong on a wedding day, which cannot be ignored. Most of the problems which can arise have been covered in this book, and solutions given, so you now know how easy the whole thing is. If any other small problems arise, just ignore them. Sometimes Bridesmaids (notoriously Grooms' sisters) can feel a bit over-shadowed and can become a little awkward as a result, but this is the sort of problem a wise Bride will ignore. If you make an issue out of it, the problem will become an argument, it can then come to light in front of two complete families, which will then lead to everyone taking sides – and this is the way family divisions and wars start!

DANCING IN YOUR WEDDING DRESS

If you have a train on your wedding dress you should have tape loops attached to the train and underskirt. When dancing, these loops slip over the wrist, so that you can 'carry' your train. Whenever you are surrounded by a lot of people, make sure you pick up your train (except in church). Too many times I have seen a guest step on the Bride's train, which rips the skirt from the bodice, which means that the Bride has to return home immediately to change, which is such a pity if this happens before the Reception.

Leaving the Reception

TAKING LEAVE OF YOUR GUESTS

If you are having a really small reception, then it may be possible to go round and kiss each of your guests 'Goodbye'. However, with a large number of guests this is not really possible, so before you go you should thank everyone who has helped you. Anyone who helped with the catering, cake, cars, music, dresses, flowers who is there. The groom can even use the D.J.'s microphone to give a short speech wishing everyone goodbye, but these special 'goodbyes' still need saying. Also anyone who has come a long distance or who is of very great age (grandparents, greatgrandparents, etc.) and any guests who cannot leave their seats through infirmity. However, the most important people to say 'Goodbye' to are your parents. Arrange for the Best Man to organise your parents to be either nearest the door, or nearest your car as you leave and try to get a few moments alone with them. If they are outside the door of the Reception, then the Best Man could close the doors as you go through them, asking the guests to wait for a few minutes, whilst you say goodbye to your parents. Most guests will understand the personal and private nature of such 'leave takings'. The doors to the hall can then be opened at a given signal (a knock from the Groom) so that the guests can all pile out to wave 'Goodbye'. This sort of gesture can mean a great deal to parents who have loved and cared for you all your lives and worked hard to help you to have the wedding you wanted!

AFTER THE BRIDE AND GROOM HAVE LEFT

After the Bride and Groom have left, most of the guests will start to disappear, even if you intend the Reception to last much longer, so if you need help in clearing up the hall (this will obviously be the parents, Best Man, Chief Bridesmaid, etc.), you should ask the D.J. to announce this now, or the Best Man can, using the D.J.'s microphone. Ask guests to return all glasses on their table to the bar. Crockery cutlery, etc. should be returned to the kitchen. Ask for volunteers for washing up and sweeping. The guests will know that you have had a tiring day and will be willing to help. When people volunteer, give them something to do immediately. Never leave willing workers standing around with nothing to do, in case they think you have forgotten them and drift off home!

The Bride and Groom should *never* stay behind to clear up. This duty must always be delegated to someone else. Nothing looks sadder on a wedding day, than the Bride with a broom in her hand!

Cash/Cheques Which the Groom/Best Man needs to have with him on The Wedding Day

Service	Cheques made payable to	Amount
Church/Licence fees		
Photographer		
D.J./Disco		
Cars		
Taxis		
Staff gratuities (tips)		
Drinks (cash behind the bar)		
Florist		
Train fares		

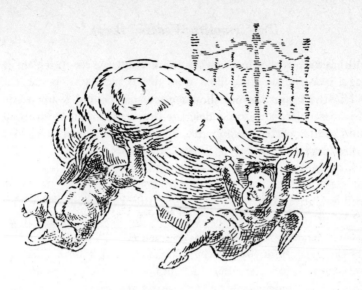

The Honeymoon

THE WEDDING NIGHT

Going Home

If, after you are married, you are going to have to have to live with your parents for a while, and you cannot afford a honeymoon, or your honeymoon does not start officially for a couple of days, try to avoid going back to your parents for the first night of your honeymoon. It is worth trying to cut back on expense elsewhere in order to afford the first night of your honeymoon somewhere other than your parents' home. It is a very bad step, psychologically. Remember you are no longer your 'mother's little girl', but it will be difficult for her to appreciate that in such a short time. And it can be embarrassing for both you and your new husband. It is probably healthier for your marriage (which is what all this is about – getting married, that is) to go without a wedding dress, rather than to spend your first night under your mother's roof.

If you are going back to a house or flat of your own, then no such problem exists, but do try to make it special. Save a bottle of champagne to take back with you. The wise groom will have bought some flowers and arranged these in a vase (a single red rose on the pillow goes down well, too) beside the bed. Most important of all, remember you might want a cup of tea or coffee and something for breakfast, so do ensure that you have tea/coffee, sugar, milk, bread, butter, marmalade. You will also need cups, knives, forks and spoons.

Most people get married on a Saturday and very few shops are open on a Sunday. Those that are open usually only stay open until lunchtime and you will be tired after the previous day, and not want to leap out of bed to go to the shops for some milk, etc.

Also think about your lunch. If you are staying at home, perhaps you could go to a restaurant for Sunday lunch. Many restaurants offer Sunday lunches at extremely reasonable rates. The day after your wedding is not the day to find out how good you are at cooking a roast! Start on Monday!

Hotels

If you have managed to afford an hotel, either just for the night, or for a longer period, do not be afraid to mention that you are honeymooners when you book their hotel. Many hotels like to know this and put champagne and flowers in the room for you. If they do not do this, then you can ask for this to be done (this is the Groom's prerogative). Also some hotels have special 'Honeymoon Suites' and it is worth enquiring as to whether they have one available.

If you feel you would like breakfast in bed, ask the desk clerk on the evening you arrive for breakfast in bed the next day. The desk clerk or receptionist will advise you about these facilities.

If you are staying at an hotel near an airport because you have an early flight the next day, ask the desk clerk to arrange an early morning call for you. The same thing applies with most hotels. You can ask for your breakfast with your call. Most hotels will only serve Continental breakfast (rolls, jam, coffee, fruit juice) at very early hours, but do not be frightened to ask. You can also order a newspaper if you like one to read before you get up.

Honeymoon Depression

After the first two or three days of marriage, some couples feel rather depressed. This often shows in the form of an argument, or else one or both becoming tearful. When abroad, many people think this is because they are homesick. Sometimes a newly wed husband with a tearful wife fears that he has done something wrong. Many girls think that what they are feeling is that something is wrong with their marriage. None of this is true. What it is, is a tremendous feeling of anti-climax! There has been a tremendous build-up to the wedding, followed by all the excitement of the wedding day, being surrounded by all your friends and family, being the centre of attention.

In most cases, your wedding day is the most exciting day of your life. After a few days, when everything starts to settle down to normal again, and there are just the two of you, on your own, it feels as though you are surrounded by a huge void and this causes the depression.

Types of Honeymoon

QUIET

The effects of honeymoon depression can be increased on very lonely honeymoons. Those Brides and Grooms who have chosen very quiet, lonely cottages to stay in on their honeymoon have found that far from being romantic, they found the whole thing rather lonely and end up spending all their time in the local pub. Of course you are going to want to spend some time on your own, but generally speaking wherever you go, guests leave honeymooners on their own in hotels, until the honeymooners make their first approach, so if you want company, you should go out and find it. Think very carefully about the sort of things that you enjoy doing together before booking a cottage which is miles away from any amenities. If you both love to ramble the countryside, then this is the right honeymoon for you, but if you like to go to discos and generally enjoy being in a crowd then you may be better off in an hotel, holiday camp or even camping on a large camping site with plenty of amenities. A few days somewhere where you can really enjoy yourself is better than a fortnight of being miserable on your own.

ACTIVE

There are many types of activity holidays available, offering everything from sailing, pony trekking, hang gliding, surfing to golf and bridge. If you are both active and have always wanted to do this sort of thing, then why not take the opportunity to learn something that you can do together, but make absolutely sure that it is something you *both* want to do. Some of these sports can make you really ache for a few days.

GOING ABROAD

To fly away to the sun is, of course, the ideal honeymoon. But if you know you are sensitive to the sun, or inclined to get an upset stomach easily, do make sure that you have remedies with you to deal with these problems.

Some African, Asian and even European destinations still require Cholera and Yellow Fever inoculations. In some cases these injections can upset the patient, so these should be completed by a fortnight before the wedding.

If you are going abroad make sure you have all the right documents with you. The travel agent will tell you what these are. Remember if you need a new passport that these can take a very long time to come through during the summer months, so order one early. It will not be possible to have your name changed on your passport until after you are married. (That is if you want your name changed. You do not *have* to change your name on marriage.) If you are stuck for a passport and you are travelling within the EEC (Common Market countries), then all you need is a British Visitors' passport, which can be obtained on production of two small photographs (the ones from photograph booths are sufficient, or photographers will do these) and your birth certificate. These can be obtained from any main post office while you wait.

The Honeymoon

CRUISING

Many couples save for years so that they can take a cruise for a honeymoon. However, make sure that you are a good sailor before going. Take a trip on the ferry to Boulogne one day, if necessary. There is nothing worse than spending a fortnight's honeymoon on a ship, being seasick all the time. Many young couples also find it a bit 'confined' and formal on some of the larger and more expensive cruise ships.

CAMPING

If you are planning a camping honeymoon, make sure that you both really like the idea. It is no good camping if one of you has never done it before and is not really used to 'roughing it'. If a new Bride wants to spend all her time dressed up, then a camping honeymoon is obviously not for her. A couple of days in a good hotel might be better.

HOTEL RATINGS

The Automobile Association awards stars to certain hotels. The more stars a hotel has, the more facilities if offers. Generally speaking, more stars also mean more expensive, although there are a few exceptions.

PACKAGE HOLIDAYS

Package holidays are probably the most popular choice for a honeymoon today. The package usually includes travel, hotel and all or some of your meals. These can be taken abroad or in this country. If you want to go abroad on holiday, packages are usually excellent value. However, care should be taken when selecting a holiday, because some tour operators charge more than others for exactly the same holiday. The reason for this is that some of the tour companies guarantee the hotels to take a certain number of rooms per week and consequently get a better rate from the hotels. Whereas another tour operator using the same hotel will not give the same guarantees and therefore the hotels charge them more, which gets handed onto the customer in higher prices. Consequently, you can end up on the same plane, and staying at the same hotel as someone else paying a lot more (or a lot less) than you. So check the holiday brochures very carefully. Think about what sort of eating arrangements you wish to make. Bed and breakfast only is ideal if you like to get away from your base either walking, driving or taking coach trips. In many places the local food is cheap and you can often enjoy the atmosphere of the country and learn a lot about it by searching out your own restaurants. This will guarantee that you have a chance to try local dishes.

Half board, which is bed, breakfast and evening meal is ideal for people who like to sit around the pool all day, or go out shopping, sightseeing or down to the beach, which may be some distance away, and do not wish to have to return to the hotel every few hours to eat. In most foreign countries, there are plenty of bars and restaurants or cafes on or near the beach.

Full board is usually provided where the beach and the hotel are right next to one another and it is assumed that their guests will be happy to swim and sunbathe all day. This is particularly so where the hotel stands on its own out in the wilds, where the guests would have to travel very great distances to find a restaurant and local transport is unreliable.

When you book a holiday, there is not usually any return of monies for meals which are not eaten, although if you are going on one of the tour operator's coach trips, which means you will be absent for a meal which you have booked, the hotel will usually arrange a packed lunch.

In many countries 'breakfast' means a continental type of breakfast, rolls and jam etc. and if you want a cooked breakfast, then you may have to pay extra for this. The Travel Agent should be able to tell you if this is so with the holiday you wish to book.

When you travel abroad with a Tour Company, when you reach your destination you are usually met by a coach with a courier. The courier will almost certainly be able to speak the language of the country you are visiting and is there to help you if you have any problems at all, so never be afraid to approach

him/her. He/she will also have details of local places of interest
and any trips which the Company may offer. Check out with
the travel agent whether it is cheaper or not to book these trips
in advance from this country. When booking trips, remember
to allow yourself some time off to recover. Many of these trips
are guided tours with extremely fit guides, who are used to
walking around all day in the heat. They can be very helpful and
informative, but it can be exhausting and if you tackle too many
trips you may find that you return more tired than when you left.

Lastly, beware of foreign water. In some European countries
it is 'safe' to drink the local water. That means that the water
has been purified and you cannot catch anything deadly from
it, but you may still get a stomach disorder from unaccustomed
chemicals which may be in the water, so it is advisable not to
drink unboiled water, but instead to buy bottles of mineral water
which are always available on request and are cheap to buy.

HONEYMOON	
Taxis	£
Wedding Night Hotel	£
Breakfast	£
Taxis/Bus	£
Trains	£
Flights	£
Ferry	£
Ship	£
Hotel/Apartment/Camp fees	£
Car Hire	£
Petrol	£
Food/Meals	£
Insurance: Car	£
Health	£
Passports	£
Trips	£
Hire of Special Equipment (skis, etc.)	£
TOTAL	£

FINAL COST				
ITEM	**TOTAL COST**	**DEPOSIT PAID**	**BALANCE DUE**	**DATE DUE**
Church Licence Hall Stationery Photographer Cars Flowers Cake Catering Appearance Honeymoon Contingency Fund				
Total £				

The Return

Whether you have been abroad, stayed in this country, or spent your honeymoon at home, there comes a time when you have to get back to reality. If you have been abroad, try to arrange your holidays with your employers, so that you have a few days at home to get yourself organised before your return to work. For one thing if you have been away, there will be washing and ironing to do. If you are lucky enough to have a washing machine, then perhaps your husband can do the washing whilst you iron, or vice versa.

You will also have to unpack and store all your wedding presents whilst still keeping note of who sent what.

Thank You Letters
Wording for thank you letters is given in the 'Stationery' section. If you now find that you had intended to hand-write your letters, but you do not have the time to do so, it will only take about fourteen days for the printed ones to come through so it may be an idea to order some of these, rather than delay the sending of 'thank you' letters any longer.

Photography

Whether your photographer brought your photographs back on your wedding day or put them in the post, your parents should have been able to have a good look at them by now. If the photographer is to bring the photographs back on your wedding day, the best thing to do is to leave them with one of the parents for a week, so that they can show them round their side of the family for a week, passing them to the other set of parents the following week, so that their side of the family can see them. You should then be able to have your photographs back on your return from honeymoon to show your friends, leaving you with plenty of time to select your own photographs and get the order to the photographer within a month (the period of time most photographers give you in which to get your orders to him).

Remember to ask your parents and friends to give you the money for the orders that they take and for their own orders. Few photographers will provide photographs without receiving the money in advance and if there are a large number of orders, then it can work out very expensive for you to have to pay the bill out of your own money.

Money

The biggest problem most Brides and Grooms face on their return from honeymoon is money. Most seem to overspend on the honeymoon, totally forgetting that when they get back they will have to eat, and the bills will be coming in by then. If you know that you are inclined to write out cheques too easily and are likely to come back from honeymoon broke, then leave some cash with one of your fathers. You may also have some money left in your 'Contingency Fund' mentioned in the first Chapter, which will help you over these first few weeks of married life.

Press Announcements

If you want a photograph in the paper, it is usually necessary for you to choose a photograph on the day of your wedding for entry in the newspaper, but if you have not done this then, you should do so immediately on return from honeymoon. Contact your photographer for details of how to go about this. It varies in different areas.

Index

Page numbers in **bold** refer to cost tables, recipes, menus and other lists.

Index

Index

Index

Index

Index